Group Therapy Techniques with Children, Adolescents, and Adults on the Autism Spectrum

Group Therapy Techniques with Children, Adolescents, and Adults on the Autism Spectrum

Growth and Connection for all Ages

Kevin B. Hull

JASON ARONSON
Lanham • Boulder • New York • Toronto • Plymouth, UK

Published by Jason Aronson
A wholly owned subsidiary of Rowman & Littlefield
4501 Forbes Boulevard, Suite 200, Lanham, Maryland 20706
www.rowman.com

10 Thornbury Road, Plymouth PL6 7PP, United Kingdom

British Library Cataloguing in Publication Information Available

Library of Congress Cataloging-in-Publication Data

Hull, Kevin B., 1971- author.
Group therapy techniques with children, adolescents, and adults on the autism spectrum : growth and connection for all ages / Kevin B. Hull.
p. ; cm.
Includes bibliographical references and index.
ISBN 978-0-7657-0933-2 (cloth : alk. paper) -- ISBN 978-0-7657-0934-9 (electronic)
I. Title. [DNLM: 1. Asperger Syndrome--therapy. 2. Autistic Disorder--therapy. 3. Psychotherapy, Group--methods. WS 350.8.P4]
RC553.A88
616.85'8832--dc23
2013032895

∞™ The paper used in this publication meets the minimum requirements of American National Standard for Information Sciences Permanence of Paper for Printed Library Materials, ANSI/NISO Z39.48-1992.

Printed in the United States of America

This book is dedicated to the amazing individuals on the autism spectrum that I have had the honor and privilege of knowing and working with over the years. You dare take the road less traveled each day and you inspire me to continue to learn, teach, write, and counsel; as you live, so I learn. I am truly grateful.

And to Wendy . . . life is so short for a love so strong.

Contents

Acknowledgments

I am deeply indebted to Amy King, Meaghan White, Kelly Blackburn, and the Rowman & Littlefield staff for helping this manuscript take on a book form. Thank you for your tireless efforts and for guiding me through this process.

—Dr. Kevin B. Hull

Chapter One

Group Therapy and the Autism Spectrum

A New Dawn

A GROUP THERAPY EXPERIENCE

Five boys, each about the same age, enter the therapy room accompanied by their therapist and sit cross-legged on the floor. The therapist, smiling at each boy, grabs a purple bouncy ball and says, "Let's begin!" The therapist hands the ball to one of the boys who takes it and says his name and begins to tell a story about something interesting that happened to him that week. The boy shares how his family is moving and that he is sad to leave his old house but feels excited to go to a new house and says his family is tired from all the work. When he is finished, he looks at a boy across the room, calls his name, and tosses the ball to him. This boy catches the ball, says his name, and also tells about an incident that happened to him earlier in the week. The boy shares his sister has been picking on him and causing him all sorts of grief; he wants to know if anybody else has a sister that is as annoying as his little sister. One boy remarks that his sister is so annoying that she makes him cry sometimes. The boy who talked about his annoying sister looks around the room and calls out another boy's name and tosses him the ball.

Six awkward adolescents are sitting in chairs placed in a circle. The therapist has given them a feelings list and they have circled various feelings that relate to the topic for that day. The therapist invites anyone who wants to talk about what they have circled to do so. One very shy young man raises his hand and quietly says, "I'll go." After a few minutes of silence, he begins to talk about feeling "rusty," "like an old tractor you see sitting in a field" he says quietly. He elaborates more; a feeling of being unwanted, unusable, and broken. A few of the others nod their heads. The therapist praises the young man for sharing and then asks if anyone else wants to take a turn. Silence. After a few minutes another young person begins to share about her feelings of being "invisible," but shares that she "kind of likes it" most of the time and he wonders aloud if that is a bad thing. No one responds but there is a feeling of connection in the silence.

Four adults sit in a room with a therapist and play the game "Catch-Phrase." Laughter and excitement erupt from the group members as they join in the game; one member struggles to explain "breast implants" to his teammates and both teams explode in laughter when they realize the answer after the buzzer sounds. The game continues and the members become very competitive as each tries very hard to help their team win. The therapist uses the experience of working together through a fun activity to help the members become more comfortable being in a group setting and allowing the parts of their personalities that are usually kept hidden to come out. As the session ends, each member continues to laugh and each has a big smile on their faces as they gather their belongings to leave. "We definitely want to play that again!" one member remarks to the therapist as he walks out the door and into the hallway.

Each of these scenarios represent a different group setting with different age groups but each group has a common theme. All of the members have been diagnosed with Asperger's Syndrome (AS) or have traits common to High Functioning Autism (HFA), which are now combined under the label Autism Spectrum Disorder (ASD). ASD disrupts these individuals' ability to connect to others as well as causing problems with self-awareness. The first group contains young children who are using the ball as a fun way to practice social conversation; the ball represents a picture of how neurotypical individuals (those who are not on the autism spectrum) naturally learn conversation. One person makes a comment and then "tosses" that comment (represented by the ball) over to someone else or drops it in the middle of the group for someone to pick up, comment, and send the ball to someone else. These young children have difficulty communicating in the typical way so the therapist is helping to give each member a picture of how conversation works. By calling each other by name, relationships are being built and social connections are being made; the members begin to take on shape and form, gradually turning into real people instead of random shapes and objects.

The second group contains adolescents who have been victims of severe bullying because of the odd and peculiar ways in which he or she behaves as a result of ASD traits. Many people diagnosed with ASD tend to have difficulty understanding his or her emotions and interpreting the emotions of others. Trauma that results from bullying wreaks further damage in the young person diagnosed with ASD not only because of the emotional problems, but because the young person can become more withdrawn, more confused, and more likely to attribute his or her awkwardness negatively towards themselves. This group experience connects the young people to other people like themselves who have experienced similar events. The group also helps each member understand and identify emotions, and to learn to express feelings and stand up for themselves.

The third group contains young adults who have struggled to find their way transitioning into adult life following high school. Those who received special services have found that there is little available for them once they become adults. All of them still live with their parents because of the difficulties that ASD brings, and the group provides them with an opportunity to connect with others who are like them and to learn to express his or her thoughts and feelings and to increase self-awareness. The group members all have difficulty with conversation; most simply shut down when asked a question, or they struggle to find an answer. The therapist has introduced the game "CatchPhrase" as a way to help the members practice spontaneous speech without overthinking each response. Activities such as this also serve as a way to build connection, self-awareness, and improve social skills for these young adults who desperately wish to find their place in the world. Through group game play, the members also experience excitement, laughter, and fun. This group also teaches these young adults to manage stress and to learn to not fear the future; instead, the members receive encouragement to find their place in the world.

WHY GROUP THERAPY?

I discuss later in the book in detail some of the latest research regarding the effectiveness of group therapy, but I will give a quick overview here. Group therapy has many benefits in helping children, adolescents, and adults in overcoming a myriad of problems. Dealing with social issues, emotional issues, and learning skills to overcome destructive patterns of living such as addiction are a few of the areas in which group therapy has been proven to be useful. There are countless research studies that support group therapy and the effectiveness of group work has been known for many years. For children, adolescents, and adults that are diagnosed with ASD, group therapy can be extremely beneficial by providing not only needed social skills, but can be an effective way of helping these individuals with issues such as low self-worth, depression and anxiety, as well as increasing coping skills to help reduce stress. Humans are programmed to be social creatures, and the group therapy setting simulates the context within which most individuals' daily lives take place. I have found that group therapy for individuals diagnosed with ASD has many benefits in addition to teaching social skills.

Group therapy provides a way to reach several individuals with the same problem at one point in time. A therapist can maximize effectiveness by providing insight and delivering techniques to several individuals at once; the group phenomenon not only provides a sense of connection mentioned above, but also can facilitate greater psychological, social, and emotional growth than individual work. This characteristic of group therapy makes it more cost effective as well. Individual sessions can be expensive, especially for families that do not have health insurance coverage, and a therapist's time is limited; therefore group therapy affords the therapist to offer services at a reduced rate while still maximizing full therapeutic benefit.

A final benefit of group therapy is that for some issues, group work has been found to be more beneficial than individual work. Group therapy connects people but adds another dimension of peer support and connection. It is the idea that the person sitting next to me may have things worse off than me. I meet other people who are also struggling and there is the sense that if that person can make it through a difficult situation then I too can find the strength to go on. This camaraderie produces a positive attitude and allows a person to reframe a problem in a more positive light. Isolation can breed feelings of being overwhelmed and discouragement which can lead to a person giving up. Connecting with others who are going through the same set of circumstances creates a strengthening of resolve. For individuals diagnosed with ASD, it may appear that isolation is preferred but in many cases I have found just the opposite. These individuals desire connection, but many have been rejected socially for so long they are simply so discouraged by the process that they have resorted to giving up. Groups provide encouragement; groups provide a sense of safety; groups provide a place that sends the message, "You are valuable and accepted, and you will not be judged or rejected."

Groups are important because they provide a place of safety and camaraderie for children, teens, and adults diagnosed with ASD. This sense of "safety" is very important for these individuals because for many of them, their brains do not interpret a social situation as being "safe." For these individuals, too many people means too many threats and too many variables to control all at once, so it is easier for the individual to avoid places where there are large crowds. A group, however, can be a "safe" place to observe, interact, and see other people "like me" who have the same interests, mannerisms, and characteristics. Perhaps the greatest aim of the groups I conduct is simply to give the group members the impression that they are not "weird," "broken," "damaged," or "unlovable;" and to help them see the amazing gifts and abilities they have because of ASD and that they *are* lovable and most of all, valuable. One of the greatest joys I have experienced as a therapist is to observe a young person who previously functioned in a shutdown and withdrawn state as a result of a lack of self-awareness and low self-worth. He emerged from these shadows and experienced connection and acceptance in the group setting. It is with this vision in mind that I have written this book.

Connor's Group Therapy Experience

Connor is a seventeen-year-old-male who was diagnosed with AS at the age of seven. Much of his childhood was spent in complete isolation from peers as he had difficulty tolerating social settings that were not familiar to him. He suffered relentless bullying as a result of appearing so different, and attending school on a regular basis became so difficult for him that his parents finally resorted to home-schooling by the seventh grade. Connor displays many of the outward characteristics of AS: little eye contact, a stiff and uncomfortable body appearance, a seeming lack of interest in the conversations of others, and a relatively unchanging facial expression. At times, Connor gazes out at the world around him; however, he does not make any conversation nor does he acknowledge anyone else's conversation. It appears as if Connor is in his own world. Connor's parents state their interest in group counseling stems from the desire to help Connor become as independent as possible but also to learn to better connect with others. While Connor's parents believe they had no choice but to shield him from the emotional and psychological damage which was occurring because of the bullying, they, like other parents who are in the same predicament, now wonder if they protected him too much and created a "social handicap."

Connor appeared very uncomfortable and stiff in the first group meeting. The others spoke to him and he did not respond, sitting on the sofa and staring out the big glass window at the lake that was just outside. The therapist let the others know that Conner was joining them today and the therapist formally welcomed Conner and reminded him that he did not have to speak if he did not want to, and went over a few other "rules" of the group. Conner did not speak during his first group experience and the attempts of the therapist to connect with him and invite him to share were met with silence as Conner simply stared out the window. The therapist waited a moment for Conner to respond after he was spoken to, and then the therapist said, "That's okay, Conner, you join us when you are ready," and moved on to the next person.

Following basic introductions, the therapist had the group play a game similar to charades. Each member took a folded piece of paper on which was written a scenario to be played out such as ordering food at a restaurant, asking for directions to a new place, or responding to someone who is angry. Each person acted out the scenario and then the situation was discussed as a group and each member shared their emotional reaction to the scenario, which ranged from fear to frustration. Conner briefly became interested in the game and the therapist noticed that he was observing the activity intensely but he did not choose to join the game and offered no verbal interaction. At the end of the group, Connor appeared relieved that the group had ended. The therapist thanked him for coming and told Conner that he hoped that he would come again. Connor made no eye contact and abruptly brushed past the therapist, briskly walking to the front door.

Evaluation of Conner's Group Therapy Experience

A casual observer would probably come to the conclusion that Conner's first group therapy experience was unproductive and that group therapy is not something that Conner is ready for. However, those who work with individuals diagnosed with ASD find this is not an uncommon occurrence and, in fact, there were some positive things that happened in this scenario. First, Conner was able to tolerate his initial anxiety despite it causing him to feel uncomfortable and actually stayed in the room. This may seem like a small accomplishment, but as someone who encounters people diagnosed with ASD often, I can tell you that this is a wonderful first step. While Conner chose not to speak, his presence indicated that in many ways, he indeed was participating. Conner came, sat, and stayed for the whole session. This is remarkable and communicates a great deal about Conner's ability to be present, even in new situations. Second, there were instances where the therapist noted that Conner was keenly observing the activity of the group, even though it seemed he was just looking out the window. It is important to never discount a person's involvement because he or she did not talk. Third, when the other group members made efforts to talk to Conner but got no response, the other members did not lash out in anger or reject him. Each one simply accepted Connor's choice to not respond and continued to participate in the group activity. The members' kindness and consideration to Conner indicated to the therapist that the members had gained new skills, while sending the message to Conner that he was welcome and there was no pressure or judgment from the members for Conner to do anything other than to just be present. The combined actions of the therapist and group members served to lay a foundation of a sense of safety for Conner that would later become very important.

I will discuss later in the book how therapists who work with individuals diagnosed with ASD need to throw out the mentality of judging whether something is positive or negative, successful or unsuccessful. While treatment goals and objectives are useful in keeping the therapy on task with a clear focus, working with individuals diagnosed with ASD does not fall into neat "boxes." Working with these individuals on the autism spectrum is a process that requires empathy and patience. It may take an individual four sessions before they join in the group experience, and that is fine because, once again, someone's mere presence is a form of participation. One of the many questions I am asked by students is "Do you *make* someone participate who chooses not to, or let them decide when they are ready?" A great question for sure, and I will address it in detail later. I believe strongly that a child, adolescent, or adult diagnosed with ASD should not and cannot be *forced* to join in a group's activities and I simply make the invitation and allow the individual to warm up, however long that may take, and wait for the individual to become comfortable with the group. If an individual is disruptive or seeking to cause harm to a group member that is another matter altogether and I may remove the person, but I do not force or punish an individual diagnosed with ASD in my groups who is not actively participating. As long as the child, adolescent, or adult is physically present that is all that I ask of them in the beginning. In my experience, once the individual is comfortable, he or she usually joins the activities and I see this as growth. I think attempting to force them would be damaging in the long run.

Conner Revisited

Conner returned to the group. In fact, at the second meeting he actually spoke. After four or five meetings, he was speaking quite a bit and joining in the activities on a regular basis. He shared with me after a year or so that the group was something that he looked forward to and that it meant a lot to him. The group not only helped Conner with social skills, but gave him a place to share about himself and allowed others his age to listen to him. The other members were fascinated by his knowledge of various topics that ranged from medieval history to movie facts, and he proved to be a very deep and philosophical thinker. I have become familiar with Conner, and like many individuals diagnosed with ASD, it takes him a short time to adjust to a new place or social situation. Through participating in the group however, this has gotten much easier for him and has even gotten him thinking about the next phase of life that will include college or finding a full-time job.

A NEW DAWN

This is an exciting time to be working with individuals diagnosed with ASD. While many new cases are being diagnosed at great rates, there is new information available that will help professionals gain a better understanding of this complicated world. There is a great need for professionals who possess patience, empathy, and skill in helping these extraordinary individuals learn to accept and understand themselves, and find a place to fit in the world. Group therapy for children, adolescents, and adults diagnosed with ASD provides important social, psychological, and emotional growth opportunities in a social context that resembles the real world. This book will provide you with valuable knowledge and skills in using group therapy with this population and add a new dimension to your therapeutic repertoire. It is my passion to bring to you, the reader, that which I have learned and used and to help you connect with children, adolescents, and adults diagnosed with ASD through the group therapy experience.

Chapter Two

Clinical Information and Additional Characteristics of Autism Spectrum Disorders

A BRIEF HISTORY

I discuss in my book, *Play Therapy and Asperger's Syndrome: Helping Children and Adolescents Connect, Grow, and Heal through the Art of Play*, a brief history of Asperger's Syndrome and how it became part of the mainstream clinical landscape. I feel that it is important for clinicians and students alike to understand the events behind this journey, not only because it is interesting, but because the history helps shed light on some important characteristics of Asperger's Syndrome and high-functioning autism (now ASD) that can sometimes be forgotten. The journey began with Hans Asperger, a Viennese pediatrician who, in 1944 published a paper that described a group of male children that had difficulty with social and emotional integration. He also noted that the children exhibited "egocentric preoccupation with unusual and circumscribed interests" (Weber, 2008, p. 15), and exhibited a conversational style that contained elements of repetitive, straightforward elements that lacked reciprocity. In the same year, Leo Kanner, a child psychiatrist, also wrote a paper describing children similar to those described in Asperger's work. Asperger's paper and the knowledge and observations it contained remained virtually ignored outside of the German scientific community until 1981 when Lorna Wing (1981) described it in a paper, and it was not until 1991 that Asperger's entire paper was translated into English by Uta Frith (1991). Curiously, Kanner's work was translated into English almost immediately after it was written and quickly spread throughout the scientific world.

Attwood (1998, 2007) and Bromfield (2010) provide interesting summaries of the research of Kanner and Asperger. There is much speculation about why these two men, who purportedly never met, did not cross paths and yet published two papers in the same year on virtually the same type of children and made similar observations. While this remains a mystery, what is known is that Kanner and Asperger helped bring to the world an organized, well documented, and well researched picture of misunderstood children whose struggles did not have a name prior to Kanner's and Asperger's papers. Asperger in particular demonstrated empathy and understanding in his connection with the children that he sought to help. Kanner included a small section at the end of his paper in which he speculated that the condition that he was observing was related to a lack of emotional connection of the parents, something that the psychological community held to for many years and can be noticed in Bettelheim's writings many years later (Bromfield, 2010).

Asperger's research was especially painstaking; he gathered teacher and parent reports and conducted intelligence testing which led him to notice the children's high performance on solving puzzles and recitation of facts, in addition to the children performing poorly on tasks that related to understanding social situations. Bromfield (2010) notes that Asperger's treatment of the parents of the children he was studying was "modern, enlightened, and sympathetic (p. 3), which I find particularly interesting. Asperger keenly noted that the traits he was observing in the children were also present in one or both of the parents. One of my passions in working with this population is to encourage parents and strengthen family connections, as well as creating support systems for those on the front lines of raising a child or adolescent diagnosed with ASD. I find it fascinating that Asperger showed great compassion for the parents and I am saddened to think that for many years it was the parents, particularly mothers, who were blamed for the struggles and challenges of children on the autism spectrum.

Uta Frith's translation of Asperger's original paper into English in 1991 generated an immediate, worldwide impact on clinicians and parents (Frith, 1991). Frith's translation and Lorna Wing's clinical work were instrumental in the inclusion of AS in both the DSM-IV and ICD-10 in 1994, (Volkmar, Klin, Siegel, Szatmari, Lord, & Campbell, 1994) and gave AS inclusion in the autistic spectrum. The information that grew from Frith's translation and Wing's work can be seen by the proliferation of articles about AS, which grew from just two publications in 1981 to over 900 by 2004 (Wing, 2005). This proliferation of information has been helpful in training therapists, counselors, and educators to work with children, adolescents, and adults who have been diagnosed with AS. A simple search on the internet will reveal large amounts of information on AS and countless websites have sprung up designed to help the professional clinician, the struggling family, or the average lay person better understand the world of AS.

AUTISM SPECTRUM DISORDER CLINICAL CONSIDERATIONS

The new revision of the DSM (DSM-V, 2013) changed some of the clinical criteria of ASD. As previously mentioned, all of the previous disorders are kept under the ASD umbrella. Some of the new changes include:

- To be diagnosed, the person must have displayed the symptoms starting in early childhood;
- The symptoms must impair the individual's ability to function in day-to-day life.

In addition, all three of the following characteristics must be present:

- *Problems reciprocating social or emotional interaction.* This includes problems with joint attention and sharing in back and forth conversations, difficulty in initiating conversation or contact with others, as well as expressing emotions and understanding the emotions of others.
- *Severe problems maintaining relationships.* This includes ignoring others, problems engaging in pretend play and interacting with peers in social events and activities, and difficulties in demonstrating appropriate behavior in different social situations.
- *Non-verbal communication problems.* This includes abnormalities in the areas of making eye contact, socially appropriate gestures and voice tones, and the inability to recognize or understand non-verbal behaviors from others.

Regarding the area of repetitive and restrictive behaviors, two of the following behaviors must be displayed:

- Extreme attachment to routines and patterns and resistance to changes in routines;
- Repetitive speech or movements;
- Intense and restrictive interests;
- Difficulty integrating sensory information or strong seeking or avoiding behavior of sensory stimuli.

Practitioners such as Bromfield (2010) and Attwood (2007), as well as myself, prefer the criteria of Gillberg (1991) over the DSM criteria that were used in the past. Many who work closely with individuals diagnosed with AS believe that the DSM criteria is lacking because it does not include the speech and language difficulties that Hans Asperger noted in his original work. Bromfield (2010) shares how Gillberg's criteria is easier to remember, is less formal, and leaves one less discouraged which the DSM tends to do, and I agree wholeheartedly. While I do not want to get into a debate regarding diagnostic criteria I do want to include the criteria of Gillberg (1991) because I believe it is important to include the sections regarding speech and language difficulties that are common in individuals diagnosed with ASD. The following is the criteria for Asperger's Syndrome that Gillberg (1991) proposed. While this criterion is intended for Asperger's Syndrome, I believe that it is still relevant and helpful for the ASD of today.

1. Severe impairment in reciprocal social interaction (at least two of the following)
    a. Inability to interact with peers
    b. Lack of desire to interact with peers
    c. Lack of appreciation of social cues
    d. Socially and emotionally inappropriate behavior
2. All-absorbing narrow interest (at least one of the following)
    a. Exclusion of other activities
    b. Repetitive adherence
    c. More rote than meaning
3. Imposition of routines and interests (at least one of the following)
    a. On self, in aspects of life
    b. On others
4. Speech and language problems (at least three of the following)
    a. Delayed development
    b. Superficially perfect expressive language
    c. Formal, pedantic language
    d. Odd prosody, peculiar voice characteristics
    e. Impairment of comprehension including misinterpretations of literal or implied meanings
5. Non-verbal communication problems (at least one of the following)
    a. Limited use of gestures
    b. Clumsy/gauche body language
    c. Limited facial expression
    d. Inappropriate expression
    e. Peculiar, stiff gaze

6. Motor clumsiness: poor performance on neurodevelopmental examination

Additional Characteristics Expanded Upon

In addition to the clinical criteria, there are other characteristics that accompany ASD that I feel are important to include in this section to help give the reader a wider view of ASD. These will be addressed specifically later in the book.

Specified Interests

An important characteristic to discuss is preoccupation with special interests. Children, adolescents, and adults diagnosed with ASD show great intensity and preoccupation with specified interests. Many of the young people and adults I encounter can talk about the things he or she loves for hours and hours, and tend to know the tiniest details about the specified interest. These interests range from television shows and movies to video games and other interests such as building models. I have encountered some individuals who are passionate about specialized interests that are uncommon such as alarm systems, antique radios, and the life cycle of earthworms and various insects.

Odd Conversation Style

Another additional characteristic that may accompany the individual diagnosed with ASD is a stiff, plodding, one-sided conversation style that appears different from a neurotypical conversation style. Neurotypical individuals tend to engage in shared conversation which usually goes like this: A person speaks and shares an idea and another person or persons hears the idea, comments on it, and then shares an idea that builds on the original idea. This goes back and forth like a tennis match until there are no more ideas to be shared or a resolution is reached and another topic is begun. A conversation with an individual diagnosed with ASD however, can appear much different. For example, the individual diagnosed with ASD may ramble on and on, not pausing to let the other person or persons comment and may appear at times rude or uncaring. This is most certainly not the case, as these individuals are not uncaring or intentionally rude; in fact, I have encountered many who are sharing very intensely because he or she actually does like me. If the person did not like me, he or she would not speak to me at all. As you can imagine, this takes some getting used to. It is important for the therapist to first build a relationship with the child, adolescent, or adult diagnosed with ASD to learn their communication style in order to understand what form of communication will work best. For example, some of the young people and adults I work with are very shy and do not demonstrate the one-sided style of communication that is a hallmark of many individuals diagnosed with ASD.

Empathy Restriction

Another characteristic that can accompany individuals diagnosed with ASD is the appearance of a lack of empathy for others' feelings. I often hear from parents/caregivers and siblings that the young person or adult diagnosed with ASD is "rude," "inconsiderate," "doesn't even care." I remind them that for neurotypical individuals what may seem as being "nice" is actually "lying" to the individual diagnosed with ASD. For example, a neurotypical child who responds to every question with "yes, ma'am/no ma'am" or "yes, sir/no, sir" might be perceived as "polite" by adults around him or her, but the child may simply be repeating a rote response without a true sense of respect for his or her elders. The child diagnosed with ASD may appear to be disrespectful by not responding in such a manner; however, he may actually have more integrity than the aforementioned child because the child diagnosed with ASD does not want to say something he does not actually believe. I worked with one young man who was bewildered as to why he should tell a host or hostess that he enjoyed the meal when he really thought it was not very good. I admire this type of integrity in these individuals; however, I do believe we must teach these young people what behavior and responses are expected in certain social situations. I will discuss this later in the book and also explain how group therapy can help individuals diagnosed with ASD understand the social "games" of the neurotypical world.

Pessimistic World View

An additional symptom that often exists in individuals diagnosed with ASD is a negative, pessimistic world view. Due to seeing the world in "black and white," these individuals tend to "call it as they see it." This can take caregivers, teachers, and peers by surprise as the young person or adult diagnosed with ASD voices a downbeat and depressing view of how they see life. I have sat in therapy sessions completely at a loss as to how to help the person sitting before me find a ray of hope of happiness, and yet, like Munro (2010) encourages, the therapist often has to be a "champion of optimism" in a form that is "just short of annoying" (p. 87). Group therapy can be a powerful force in helping to be a source of encouragement and hope for these amazing individuals.

Mindblindness and Alexithymia

Mindblindness and alexithymia are two characteristics of ASD that cause a great deal of difficulty for individuals on the autism spectrum. Mindblindness is a term that describes the inability of the person diagnosed with ASD to see a situation from another person's perspective, and creates difficulty in predicting the intentions or motives of others (Baron-Cohen, 1995). Mindblindness results in a lack of empathy and disrupts the ability of the person diagnosed with ASD from using his or her imagination to connect with others' feelings and to interpret those feelings. I will be discussing mindblindness throughout the book, particularly in the section where I discuss how group therapy can improve perspective-taking in the individual diagnosed with ASD. The characteristic of mindblindness is common in those individuals on the autism spectrum, but I am one who believes that with practice and help, individuals can learn to develop what is known as Theory of Mind (ToM), the ability to see a situation or envision a concept from another's perspective. McGuire and Michalko (2011) present an alternative viewpoint of mindblindness and state that while it is a common characteristic of those on the autism spectrum, mindblindness is in fact an element of communication among neurotypical individuals as well. In essence, everyone, whether diagnosed with ASD or not, can display the effects of mindblindness at one time or another.

Alexithymia is known as the "inability to recognize and give meaning to emotional signals in oneself and others" (Hull, 2011, p. 16). Fitzgerald and Bellgrove (2006) discuss how alexithymia is a common characteristic for those diagnosed with ASD. Alexithymia causes a great deal of difficulty in forming relationships with others because the individual diagnosed with ASD has a hard time "reading" the emotions of others, which results in confusion for the person on the autism spectrum and hurt feelings in those around them. For example, an adolescent diagnosed with ASD may say something inappropriate to a peer, who, naturally, will display a negative emotional reaction. The adolescent diagnosed with ASD however, does not recognize the negative emotional reaction of their peer and continues talking, but suddenly realizes that the person they were talking to has now walked away. As you can imagine, the offended person will probably avoid the person diagnosed with ASD from this moment on. Unfortunately, this scenario is all too common for individuals on the autism spectrum.

Alexithymia also disrupts the ability of the person to understand their own emotions and make sense of them. Taylor, Bagby, and Parker (1997) state that individuals who struggle with alexithymia are "unable to identify accurately their own subjective feelings, verbally communicate emotional distress to other people very poorly, thereby failing to enlist others as sources of aid and comfort" (p. 30). This means that these individuals are confused by the emotions that arise within them and this confusion often is manifested by tantrums in young children and adolescents on the autism spectrum, and depression in older individuals on the autism spectrum. Children and adolescents diagnosed with ASD struggle with frustration tolerance; for them, the slightest irritation tends to be magnified exponentially. This results in a boy who yells and throws things because his mother has told him that there is not enough time for him to play his favorite video game or a girl screams and scratches at her legs until they bleed because her favorite sweater is in the wash and she cannot wear it to school. To a neurotypical individual, the level of the outburst in relation to the trigger does not make sense; the child is reacting as if they are going to die. However, inside the child's brain and body, the reaction really is as if "I am going to die!"

Mindblindness and alexithymia create great struggles for the individual on the autism spectrum not only in the relationship-building arena, but in self-awareness as well. For these young people, the task of identity formation is made complicated by not being able to understand who he is, who she wants to be, and what he or she wants out of life. This lack of self-awareness keeps him in a state of "high alert"; her brain tends to stay in "fight-or-flight" mode. While the challenges created by alexithymia and mindblindness seem to create insurmountable obstacles for individuals on the autism spectrum, there is a great deal of research that shows these individuals are able to learn to overcome these obstacles. Group work can be a wonderful way to help an individual diagnosed with ASD learn to interpret the emotions of others, learn to recognize and communicate about his or her internal emotional states, and learn to see a situation from another person's perspective.

CONCLUSIONS: A NEW MIND-SET

This chapter contains a great deal of clinical information and my effort here is to provide the reader with a picture of the scientific community's view of what ASD is so that we, mental health practitioners, may know and understand the language of those who work in the scientific and diagnostic realm. The autism spectrum is one of those places in the medical and psychological research world that is a constantly shifting landscape. Due to continued advances in medical technology, the "mystery" of autism continues to be decoded, and new ways of studying the brain are being found and refined. New ways of studying genes and the interplay of genetics and brain chemistry are also opening up new ways of understanding the mystery of autism. Some readers may have read the previous section and wondered if there is any hope for a person diagnosed with ASD; it certainly is tempting to think in negative terms and see a young person or adult on the autism spectrum as "less than," "damaged," or "broken." Certainly, the aforementioned characteristics are quite a bundle of obstacles, but I want to challenge the reader to resist seeing these characteristics in a negative light. I am a firm believer that we must strive to see an individual's differences and characteristics in a positive light, and learn to celebrate those in a strength-based manner. For too long, traditional psychology has presented the differences of people as "disorders" and "illness" and this applies to those on the autism spectrum. I remind myself daily as I work with these amazing individuals that the very characteristics that make one of these individuals "different" is what also makes them wonderful and amazing.

Will you join me in the commitment to shift to a positive, strength-based mind-set when it comes to working with those on the autism spectrum? While I believe that it is our duty as mental health professionals to teach individuals diagnosed with ASD new skills to help him or her adapt socially and better understand him or herself, I never want to give the young person the sense that they are damaged or broken. I definitely want to educate the individual diagnosed with ASD about the challenges that ASD brings, but I also want to instill hope and the sense that I am providing skills and tools to help them adapt, not change who they are. In addition, I am also passionate about helping the young person understand who he or she is and accept the characteristics ASD brings. There is no greater joy for me than when one of the young people that I work with finds that his or her intensity can be channeled towards a positive place and that the passion that he or she has for something can be transferred towards a career path or a hobby that brings them a sense of fulfillment. As we now move into exploring how group therapy can be beneficial for those diagnosed with ASD, bring this new mind-set with you and prepare to enter an exciting new way to help individuals diagnosed with ASD overcome these obstacles.

Chapter Three

Effectiveness and Usefulness of Group Therapy

Group Therapy has a long and rich history. This section of the book will examine a brief overview of the evolution of group therapy and the effectiveness of group therapy in general. Finally, a discussion of how group therapy can be used with individuals diagnosed with ASD and therapist characteristics will be presented.

THE EFFECTIVENESS OF GROUP THERAPY

Yalom (2005) cites eleven "therapeutic factors" (p. 1) that uphold the effectiveness of group therapy. I will review each of these briefly and demonstrate how these factors complement each other and create an interwoven tapestry that results in the group approach being a strong and dependable therapeutic dynamic. The therapeutic factors are as follows:

1. Instillation of Hope
2. Universality
3. Imparting Information
4. Altruism
5. The Corrective Recapitalization of the Primary Family Group
6. Development of Socializing Techniques
7. Imitative Behavior
8. Interpersonal Learning
9. Group Cohesiveness
10. Catharsis
11. Existential Factors

Installation of Hope

Certainly, the therapeutic experience is about bringing hope to those who are hurting, feeling a sense of emptiness, and struggling to understand themselves or others. There is a good deal of research that shows a positive outcome of therapy, whether group or individual, occurs when the client is hopeful that the therapy will produce a positive outcome (Hoberman, Lewinsohn & Tilson, 1988; Irving, Snyder, Cheavens, Gravel, Hanke, Hilberg & Nelson, 2004; Snyder, Parenteau, Shorey, Kahle, & Berg, 2002). The group therapy experience instills a sense of hope in the members who are participating by providing a sense of companionship; that is, each member is encouraged to go on because of the sense of a joined struggle. Groups provide great encouragement and hope because members know that others are hurting in the same way, struggling with the same issues, and in a general sense, trying to overcome or deal with a problem that is similar. For example, a common theme in the groups that I facilitate is bullying. Most of the young people have either been bullied (some severely) or are dealing with a bullying situation at some level on a daily basis. I have witnessed time and again a young person coming to group in a defeated state because of a bullying situation and leaving in a hopeful and encouraged state because they heard of another group member dealing with the same situation. This instillation of hope provides a huge source of emotional strength that translates into coping with a very difficult situation.

Universality

Universality is the revelation that "I'm not the only one"; many people, particularly those going through great trials, tend to believe that not another person on earth could feel as bad as they do or that anyone else has it any worse. Yet, the group experience is powerful in that people realize that indeed others do have great struggles, and often, these trials are worse than those of the person who previously believed they were "the only one." This revelation instills hope, creates resilience, and gives the group members a chance to shift perspective which then encourages better coping skills. For those on the autism spectrum who struggle with seeing things from other perspectives in the first place, there is often a sense of being very much alone, and I find many of these individuals simply believe that he or she is "the only one" who is bullied, misunderstood, and rejected by others. Group therapy can be a wonderful way to help shift the individual to see a new perspective, and some of the most rewarding moments in my life as a therapist have been witnessing that very eye-opening moment when a child, adolescent, or adult is astounded to find "others" who feel like they do and struggle with the same issues.

Imparting Information

Yalom (2005) delineates two different types of teaching that groups can offer: Didactic instruction and direct advice. The first, didactic instruction takes the form of teaching people specific principles about a topic and constitutes "the initial binding force in the group, until other therapeutic factors become operative" (Yalom, 2005, p. 11). A group that provides psychoeducation, such as relaying the importance of medication compliance upon leaving an inpatient hospital, is one example of how a group may provide didactic instruction. Teaching young people on the autism spectrum how to connect with others and build friendships is another. Didactic instruction is usually delivered by a group leader or leaders, with little input from the group members. Direct advice, the second means of imparting information, describes the phenomenon in which the group members share with each other a personal view of what a certain member should do to solve their problem or dilemma they are facing. This is common in support groups and recovery groups and can be a powerful force in a person learning to accept themselves, trust others, and make changes in his or her life. For people on the spectrum, both forms of imparting information occur in groups. For example, a social skills group for young people involves the teaching of dealing with anxiety, learning the basics of conversation, and practicing how to build a friendship. Groups for people on the spectrum also involve advice giving. For example, in one group that I facilitate for adolescents, much of the time is spent brainstorming how each person can help someone else overcome their given issue or dilemma. The advice giving helps to not only encourage the one giving the advice, but also helps the listener by offering strategies that have been tried and proven to work.

Altruism

Yalom (2005) cites the importance of altruism in that "members gain through giving, not only in receiving help as part of the reciprocal giving-receiving sequence, but also in profiting from something intrinsic to the act of giving" (p. 13). Doing something for someone else, giving of oneself to help another whether through words or deeds, helps pull one out of despair. As I have written earlier, individuals on the autism spectrum struggle with seeing things from another person's perspective, but this does not mean that they are incapable of helping another person. Often, the person on the autism spectrum simply does not have the knowledge of *how* to communicate their care and concern to another person. Certainly, the group setting provides the individual on the autism spectrum with the opportunity to not only learn *how* but also to practice giving to those around them.

The Corrective Recapitulation of the Primary Family Group

Yalom (2005) states that many individuals who seek out help from a therapy group often have had negative experiences with their family of origin. While this is not always the case with individuals on the autism spectrum, it is true that for these individuals, group settings have typically been confusing and scary places. Many of the individuals on the spectrum with whom I come in contact share with me how groups represent frightening situations and that "too many people" create feelings of anxiety. The therapy group can reverse this type of thinking by providing a group experience that is positive and not scary, while at the same time give the individual diagnosed with ASD valuable skills in building their self-confidence and learning to navigate group settings. I witnessed the power of a group that is non-judgmental, totally accepting, and fun that helps transform a young person from a shy, anxious, timid person into a person who is ready and able to join groups in the "real world" based on the good experience in the therapy group.

Development of Socializing Techniques

While this seems obvious, Yalom (2005) discusses some important elements related to the socializing nature of groups that I think are important to note. First, it is through observation and practice that all human beings learn what is acceptable and what is not acceptable for group behavior. For some, particularly those on the autism spectrum, learning these cues and becoming comfortable in groups can take longer than it does for the neurotypical individual. The most popular groups for individuals on the autism spectrum, especially children, are social skills groups. I will be discussing these in later chapters when I discuss the usefulness of social skills training for children, adolescents, and adults. These groups provide the opportunity for strategic teaching, modeling, and practicing newly acquired skills. A second part of the socialization process that groups provide is the insight that is gained from other members' sharing personal stories and experiences that help create a context for greater social understanding. For example, one key element that I teach in my groups with children and adolescents is the importance of hygiene. I remember distinctly one group member who would participate in the discussion of hygiene in the group setting but this had yielded little change at home or school, much to the frustration of his family. One day, however, one of the other group members looked at him directly and told him that he smelled and needed to use deodorant. The young man was stunned and appeared to be a little hurt. I was not surprised when I heard from the mother a few weeks later that the young man had demonstrated a complete turnaround in the hygiene arena and was not only wearing deodorant but bathing and brushing his teeth on a regular basis.

Imitative Behavior

Yalom (2005) states that the role of therapist in the group provides a model for group members in which they can observe the behavior of the therapist as well as senior group members as a form of learning and incorporating what they see into their life. It is common for those in groups to attach very strongly to the group leader, especially in the early stages of the group. The group leader plays an important role in this area. The leader must be able to instill a sense of safety, as well as form a connection that will lead to trust. As this is happening, the leader must model socially appropriate behavior and be attentive to group members' emotional and mental functioning. It is no small task and requires a great deal of energy. Later chapters will discuss how the therapist can pull together all the necessary components and how imitative behavior plays an important role for those on the autism spectrum.

Interpersonal Learning

Yalom (2005) sees the dynamic of interpersonal learning as made up of three distinct factors: 1) The importance of interpersonal relationships; 2) The corrective emotional experience; and 3) The group as a social microcosm (p. 47). Each of these plays an important role in creating the whole experience of interpersonal learning. Combined, these factors explain how human relationships are necessary for survival and that in therapy groups in particular, the interpersonal relationships that evolve have the power to correct maladaptive behavior through the creation of insight for group members. The group experience provides the correct environment for healing and change to occur. For those on the autism spectrum, I would definitely concur with Yalom's assessment that all of these ingredients combine to create a powerful experience. While those on the autism spectrum do encounter challenges in relating to others, I have observed numerous times how the members of the groups that I have had the privilege of conducting often think about each other when they are away from the group and that the group experience provides a source of insight and confidence as well as a loving, learning environment that has the power to shape human behavior.

Group Cohesiveness

Group cohesiveness can be described as the feelings of trust among group members that result in a sense of togetherness and belonging. Yalom (2005) states that "cohesiveness is the group therapy analogue to relationship in individual therapy" (p. 53), and he devotes an entire chapter to the concept of group cohesiveness and explains the great deal of research that positively supports the important role of group cohesiveness. He makes the point that for many individuals, there has never been a positive experience in groups, whether in his or her family of origin or other microcosms of society. Certainly for those diagnosed with ASD, group experiences can be difficult which leave a trail of negative memories and emotions. I encounter many children, adolescents, and adults who report not only feeling inept at joining groups but also have had many negative experiences resulting in rejection by others in their neighborhoods, schools, and churches. Often, the members enter the therapy group feeling very nervous and are hesitant to interact based on previous experiences. If a group has already formed, a new member must find where he or she fits, and learn the "rules," which can seem overwhelming and frightening. However, as the therapist connects with each member (more on that later in the chapter!) and strives to create an atmosphere of safety and acceptance, the member who was once skeptical and hesitant becomes enjoined and involved and is able to benefit from the group experience.

Catharsis and Existential Factors

I have combined the last two of Yalom's (2005) therapeutic factors into one section because I believe there is significant overlap between them. Catharsis is what occurs when group members release feelings about themselves, their circumstances, and others. This process promotes insight, healing, and coping skills that enable the person to find the strength to move through a difficult situation and to keep going in an authentic, intentional, and hopeful manner. I liken it to having surgery to fix a broken or malfunctioning part of our bodies. While the experience of surgery is not pleasant and certainly involves risk factors, the end result is that the body as a whole will function better as a result of the surgical procedure performed on a certain area of the body. While releasing feelings in a group setting can be uncomfortable and downright terrifying for some individuals, the outcome of doing so can promote great healing and growth. When I discuss the overall benefits of the group therapy experience with potential members, I always end with giving the future members a picture of how the experience can benefit them.

Existential factors refer to the fundamental truths that Yalom (2005) believes summarize the "confrontation with the human condition" (p. 98): Life can be unfair and unjust; there is no escape from pain; no matter how close one gets to others one is ultimately alone; there is no escape from the inevitability of death, and by facing the realities of life and death one can live life in an honest manner and not be bogged down by insignificant pursuits or worries. These factors are the root of the anxiety that creates problems for people and yet facing this struggle also has the potential to bring meaning and purpose and peace for the human being who is willing to face them head-on. It is important to remember that individuals on the autism spectrum also struggle with the same fears and struggles of living and dying as neurotypical individuals. In fact, I have found that the characteristics of ASD can create more of a keen awareness of the reality of death and dying which can result in intensifying various fears and worries. Group therapy can certainly provide a safe environment for these existential factors to be talked about and touched upon, while at the same time giving the individual diagnosed with ASD insight and hope in dealing with the struggles of life.

HOW GROUP THERAPY CAN BE EFFECTIVE WITH THOSE ON THE AUTISM SPECTRUM

Group therapy has specific uses for those diagnosed with ASD. This section will present an overview of how the group experience can be a powerful approach for those on the autism spectrum. I have included a blend of research and personal experience in this section.

Teaching Specific Social Skills

A quick search of the internet will reveal just how popular social skills groups and social skills curriculum are for children and adolescents on the autism spectrum. Parents and caregivers are eager to seek out these groups for their young person diagnosed with ASD to help him or her become better at navigating the social world. Social skills groups have been found to be effective in helping young people learn specific social skills, such as acquiring manners, engaging in conversation, and learning how to build relationships with others (Rao, Beidel, & Murray, 2008). Because of the nature of ASD, many struggle with the basics of forming relationships. Things such as communication, approaching strangers, and knowing the structure of certain social tenets of society (i.e. standing in line, taking turns, etc.) can all be quite baffling for the individual. I often equate the struggle of the young person diagnosed with ASD to what it must be like to land on a foreign planet, but lacking the specific tools that one needs in the new environment. For example, the terrain of the new planet is marsh-like, but the new explorer only has dress shoes. The climate is cold, requiring heavy clothing with many layers, but the new explorer only has thin clothing that will not keep the person warm and comfortable. Because of this, the new explorer feels out of place, uncomfortable, and propels him or her to find shelter *away* from their current environment. So also the individual diagnosed with ASD finds that the landscape he or she is trying to traverse is confusing and terrifying, and the individuals find themselves often ill-equipped to deal with the situations found in most social settings. Thus, the individual does what comes naturally when a human being finds such an unpleasant experience: Avoid the experience or circumstance at all costs, or fight against the possibility of being thrown into it. Social skills groups are helpful because the goal is to give the individual diagnosed with ASD skills and tools to traverse the landscape of social interactions and to do so in a gradual, safe manner. I will discuss social skills groups in more detail in chapters 4, 5, and 6.

Overcoming Alexithymia

Group therapy can be helpful in overcoming the difficulties of alexithymia. I have mentioned already the struggle that many children, adolescents, and adults diagnosed with ASD have in understanding emotions and interpreting emotional signals in others. This deficit creates major problems, from behavior "meltdowns" and withdrawn, avoidant behavior to the inability to form relationships with others. Taylor, Bagby, and Parker (1997) discuss how people with alexithymia "prefer to be alone and avoid people altogether" (p. 44) and that these individuals tend to develop negative behaviors such as binge eating and developing somatic symptoms. The group setting provides the opportunity to help individuals diagnosed with ASD understand emotions, learn strategies to help express those emotions, and also learn to recognize emotional signals in others. I have found that the group setting adds an extra dimension in helping the individual diagnosed with ASD battle alexithymia for a couple of reasons. First, the individual finds that he or she is not alone in their struggle. Second, the group setting allows for the practice of recognizing emotions in others and expressing emotions to others in the group through game play or role play. Third, the group setting provides a therapist with the chance to have the individual put into practice what has been learned in the individual sessions. I will discuss specific ways that group therapy can be used in overcoming alexithymia in chapters 4, 5, and 6.

Increasing Perspective-taking

I have already discussed how the inability to see things from another's perspective, or mindblindness, causes a great deal of difficulties for the individual diagnosed with ASD. Group therapy provides excellent opportunities to help the individual diagnosed with ASD learn to see a situation from another's perspective for two reasons. The first is that the group setting creates an environment that forces the individual to be exposed to different viewpoints and perspectives. A group setting forces one to pull out of a selfish mind-set, which is certainly one of the benefits of group therapy, regardless of the type of group. For example, imagine a young boy diagnosed with ASD who absolutely hates sports. He likes nature and cannot understand why other people do not like nature as much as he does. He joins a group and there finds himself sitting next to a boy whose love of sports matches his love of nature. At first, the boy who loves nature is annoyed and thoroughly uninterested as the boy who loves sports talks about his favorite teams.

However, over time, the boys both have the opportunity to see that their passions, while different, are felt in the same way on the inside. Over time, there is the possibility for both boys to realize that others have interests and passions that are different and that this is okay. This, to me, is one of the most important elements of group therapy for those diagnosed with ASD.

A second way that group therapy can help with perspective-taking is through strategic techniques that the group leader uses to gradually help shift the members to see things from another perspective. I will be discussing these in detail in chapters 4, 5, and 6. Group therapy sessions can provide a sense of connection and safety among members which provides a wonderful foundation for applying techniques that help with perspective-taking. I have found that when a group member feels a sense of safety and camaraderie, it is easier for the individual to let down their "walls" and try to see a situation from another's perspective. Group members can also provide encouragement during this process and the therapist can also be a "cheerleader" while at the same time teaching these valuable skills.

Increasing Self-Worth and Self-Confidence

A common problem for individuals diagnosed with ASD is low self-worth. Children and adolescents who have experienced rejection by peers develop self-loathing (Carter, 2009) and Baron-Cohen (2000) found that the "residue of bullying and social rejection can become embedded into the child's internal processes which results in withdrawal, isolation, and feelings of loneliness that the child carries well into their adult years" (Hull, 2011, p. 28-29). Ghazuiddin, Ghazuiddin, and Greden (2002) found that individuals diagnosed with ASD often view themselves as less competent than their peers and feelings of low self-worth resulted from this viewpoint. Self-worth is important as it represents the foundation of "I matter" on which achievements, relationships, and the ability to develop coping skills rests. Because individuals diagnosed with ASD are often on the "sidelines" in society, it is no wonder that these amazing individuals believe that there is something wrong with them. Group therapy can be a powerful experience in helping to increase an individual's sense of self-worth through creating an environment of acceptance and freedom to explore one's abilities and attributes, resulting in a greater valuing of the self.

Ben, Mario Bros. and Self-Worth

Ben, a ten-year-old male, began attending one of the groups that I offer on a weekly basis. I had seen him in individual therapy as well, and after talking with the mother about his difficulties in social settings, I recommended giving the group sessions a try. Diagnosed with ASD since the age of five or six, Ben's self-worth was fragile; his perfectionistic tendencies and need to be in control in order for his brain to tell him he was safe created difficulties when he was in the company of others. One way in which this was manifested was in his hesitation to try anything new for fear that it would be one more "thing that I will fail at," leading him to avoid anything that he considered new or different. One of these "new" ventures was my Nintendo Entertainment System and the game Super Mario Bros. Ben was instantly drawn to it as it represented a relic of a bygone era of electronic gadgetry that absolutely fascinated him (yes, I have my original NES that was a Christmas gift in 1988, and yes, it still works and gets used almost daily!), but he was terrified to "fail." He wanted to watch me play it because he was drawn to the Mario Bros. story (Mario and Luigi, the various villains, and the bright colors of the Mario world) but any attempt to get him to play resulted in him saying "no" emphatically and then ordering me to turn it off. I could see the war that raged within this young man: on the one hand, he wanted to try playing the video game, but, on the other hand, the thought of failure terrified him because his self-worth was very fragile.

The particular group that Ben joined loved the Mario games and I used the world of Mario as a metaphor for dealing with bullying, staying positive, and even to talk about the opposite sex through the characters of Princess Peach and Princess Toadstool. Usually at the end of the group, the members would gather around the game system and the members would take turns playing through the various levels and "worlds" of one of the many Mario Bros. games. I will discuss later how video and computer games played as a group can teach perspective-taking, instill patience through turn-taking, and also give young people a chance to practice giving encouragement and teaching. Ben was amazed at the skill of the group members and was drawn to the game play, but when asked if he wanted to give the game a try, he instantly declined and stated that "he was afraid to fail." One of the group members got up and walked over to Ben and offered his controller, and told Ben "None of us were very good at the beginning, but we will teach you. Don't be afraid." The other members echoed the same sentiment and reluctantly, Ben took the controller and began to play. The first few times he attempted to maneuver his character through the world of Goombas and Piranha Plants, Ben met with failure. His response to this was exactly as I had predicted: he screamed and threw the controller down, and buried his head in the corner of the couch and began to wail and moan, rocking back and forth. The other members were shocked by Ben's behavior, but I coached them through the experience and used it as an opportunity to teach them to offer sympathy, comfort, and encouragement. The members each attempted to comfort Ben and I directed them back to the game in order to give Ben some time to cool off.

Ben was able to gather himself and after a few moments rejoined the group play, fascinated by the video game. Finally, he agreed to try again, and again, he met with failure. However, each time that he "failed" his tantrum behavior lessened and he was able to remain with the group. While he was obviously disappointed and upset with himself for not being able to achieve perfection, I saw that he was gradually learning to accept his failure and that he was able to put into a perspective that just being part of the group was fun enough. Finally, after some more attempts, Ben completed a level all by himself. I can still see him with arms in the air, yelling triumphantly, "I did it!" and the other members clapping and cheering for him. From that moment, Ben's self-worth and confidence increased, not only in his video game play, but in other areas of his life. He began to talk more and share more about himself and his mother reported that he was branching out into other areas of learning instead of isolating himself to the specified interests that he had been preoccupied with for so long.

Establishing a Sense of Identify

"Who am I" is a question that most people, whether diagnosed with ASD or not, spend a great deal of time trying to figure out. For people on the autism spectrum, the issues of identity and self-awareness are even more baffling due to the problems that I discussed previously. Having a sense of identity and being self-aware is an important task during development (Erikson, 1963) and is an important foundation of being self-sufficient and establishing relationships with others (Bell & Bell, 2005; Tuason & Friedlander, 2000). Group interaction provides individuals on the autism spectrum with opportunities to learn about whom he or she is, and teaches the person to be able to put that conceptualization into words. The development of this awareness of self has many positive benefits: increased perspective-taking, better social interactions, and a sense of independence that can lead to increased opportunities such as social awareness and employment.

There are many subcategories of identity work for those on the autism spectrum in which group therapy can be helpful. Sexual identity, a very important and emerging area of research and practice, is often overlooked by parents and practitioners when it comes to individuals on the autism spectrum. I will be discussing the application of group techniques to work on sexual identity in chapter 5. The establishment of a career and the identity process that accompanies this process is another important part of development and group therapy provides a wonderful way to aid those diagnosed with ASD in learning about who they are related to their chosen career or interest. Group therapy can even be useful in helping adults on the spectrum who are expectant parents in preparing for their new role and identity as a parent.

GROUP THERAPY FOR THOSE ON THE AUTISM SPECTRUM IS LIMITLESS!

As you can see, the benefits of group therapy are many. What I hope that you take away from this chapter, whether you are new to the field or a seasoned professional, is that group therapy is a powerful force and can be applied to nearly every issue and dynamic imaginable. Group therapy can be adapted to address the challenges that individuals diagnosed with ASD face during the developmental process. The following chapters will explain group therapy techniques for children, adolescents, and adults.

How Many? How Long? How Often?

Group Size

Some common questions for those considering conducting group therapy with individuals on the autism spectrum are related to the number of participants to include in a group, how long a group should last and how often a group should meet together to be effective. First, I want to say that there is no set answer for these questions—only that it depends on the mind-set of the therapist and the dynamics of the group. I suggest keeping the groups for children small and between three to five members. I have found that adding more than five can be counterproductive. If the children with whom you are working are lower functioning, you should consider keeping the group number at three. However, there is no magic formula. Smaller groups tend to be easier to manage from a behavior standpoint and the concepts being taught can be better absorbed if there are fewer children.

Children on the autism spectrum can be challenging in a group setting, as each one brings his or her individual characteristics that may not mesh well with another child's emotional and mental makeup. Putting five or six (or more) intense, highly intelligent, and sensitive young people who are used to doing things their way together in a space creates the potential for problems. By simply reducing the number in a group, the group leader can better manage the stress level and get more accomplished. While group leaders cannot foresee every possible problem that may cause stress, we should strive to make the group experience enjoyable and inviting. Smaller groups also allow the leader to be able to turn a stressful event for a child into a valuable learning experience. For example, Rob, a boy in one of my groups, loved smoke detectors and had a passion to find old detectors and get them working again. Steven, another group member, suffered from sound sensitivity and one thing that terrified him was the piercing sound emitted from smoke detectors and fire alarms. One day, I allowed Rob to bring a smoke detector that he had found at a garage sale that did not work. Prior to the group session I told Steven, who knew about Rob's passion for smoke detectors, that Rob was going to bring one in but that it did not work and no sound would emit from the device. Despite him telling me that he understood, as soon as Steven saw the detector he ran screaming from the room in complete terror covering his ears. I followed him and comforted him, but no amount of reasoning could help him see that the device was completely disarmed, and he refused to come back into the group room until he knew that the device was removed. Rob, who for a week was eager to show off something that meant so much to him, was devastated by Steven's reaction. The result was one terrified child and one very disappointed child, and all of this happened in less than one minute.

I use this illustration for those choosing to conduct groups with young people on the autism spectrum to demonstrate two very important points: one, things will not always go according to plan and two, be prepared to use the emotional reactions of the group members as a teaching opportunity. Despite the fact that I had Steven, who was terrified, and Rob, who was very disappointed and beginning to burst into tears, I also had a golden opportunity to help Steven work through his fear and help Rob understand his disappointment and work through it. This group only had three members, which made it easier to deal with a situation such as this and also involve the third member in the learning process. Had the group been larger, I would not have been able to attend to the immediate needs of Rob and Steven and turn a potential crisis into a learning situation.

Duration of a Group

Again, there is no formula for how long a therapy group should last. My answer to this lies in examining what goals the therapist wishes to accomplish. Due to the nature of the range of issues experienced by those on the autism spectrum, it is possible to have groups run indefinitely, but the therapist should have treatment goals so that he or she is working towards a resolution point. For example, many of the groups that I run are intended to help deal with a range of issues, from teaching social skills to dealing with emotional issues, and there is no specific time frame for the groups. However, I have a set of goals in place for each group and also a planned idea of what issues will be addressed. I personally like the idea of an ongoing group because each individual is unique. Some may take longer than others to understand the concepts and make gains. For others, the group represents the only social contact for them and is a very important part of their lives. I have witnessed the powerful effect of a warm and accepting group on a child or adolescent who, prior to joining the group, tended to see others as dangerous and wanted to avoid groups. However, there are groups which are time limited and guided by well-founded and effective principles. As mentioned earlier, there are no hard and fast rules.

Frequency of Group Meetings

A final consideration is how often a group should meet. Again, there is no magic formula. However, due to the nature of the topics and issues that will be worked on, the frequency with which a group meets does matter, especially when working with young people. Yalom (1995) recommends meeting weekly to keep the momentum of the group moving forward and to maintain connection between members. I have found that meeting weekly or at least biweekly is sufficient to keep the topics at hand fresh in the young person's mind and also to maintain the continuity of connection and relationship between members. I believe that weekly sessions are most helpful when attempting to teach strategic skills, such as overcoming grief or trauma, or teaching social skills. Too much time between groups can create heightened anxiety for the members or the members can forget what was worked on in the previous meeting, thus impeding group cohesion and momentum.

DEALING WITH EMOTIONAL OUTBURSTS AND RESISTANCE IN GROUP THERAPY WITH THOSE DIAGNOSED WITH ASD

Two final issues that are important to address are dealing with emotional outbursts and resistance in group therapy with individuals diagnosed with ASD. Individuals on the autism spectrum are unique, and because of this many can easily be triggered emotionally and mentally which can be disruptive to the group experience. Conducting group therapy with this population can be trying for the therapist who is rigid and expecting immediate results. The need for patience, compassion, and mindfulness of everyone involved is of utmost importance for the therapist attempting this work. I have conducted groups in which one action of one member triggered two other members into emotional outbursts and another to shut down. In this instance, a boy brought a device unbeknownst to me that emitted a sound that terrified two of the members, and their reaction caused the fourth member to shut down because of their shrieking. What is a therapist to do? I have an answer and it begins with the therapist being non-reactive, respectful, and always being conscious of modeling a calm, safe presence for group members regardless of their age or abilities. Just as individuals on the autism spectrum can be unpredictable, so can the course of group therapy. A therapist may find a technique that helps most of the group members, but one of the members is severely emotionally triggered by that technique and for the benefit of that one member, the therapist cannot use the technique. For example, I happened to bring in a pet guinea pig one day for group without checking with everyone and all the members were ecstatic except one boy who was completely terrified of small furry animals and ran from the room in sheer terror. Be prepared that your group members will be triggered emotionally at some point during the course of the group and be ready to attend to the needs of that person. You may need to take an upset child to a parent if you can't soothe them, or the group may need to stop for the time being to process what has happened. Remember this one rule: Use EVERYTHING that happens during the group as a way to teach regardless of how seemingly unstructured and chaotic things seem. I even turned a terrible Florida thunderstorm complete with devastating lightning and thunder into a way to help a group of very frightened boys deal with fears. I quickly gathered the members in a circle and I made up the "I'm Not Scared of You, Thunder!" song which contained phrases such as "Thunder, you're just a stupid noise and noise can't hurt anybody, you don't even have a body!" and "I hate you, Thunder, nobody loves you, and you're so mean, and I bet you're ugly if you even were real!" By the end of the group, fear had turned into laughter and joy as several of the boys overcame their fear of thunder. Because I was quick on my feet, I was able to use an actual event in real time to demonstrate how song and humor can be very effective in getting over worry and fear.You never know what will be offered to you that can be used to help group members learn new coping skills.

Chapter Four

Group Therapy with Young Children Diagnosed with ASD

I have chosen to devote two chapters to group therapy with children: Group therapy techniques for young children and group therapy techniques for older children. I have chosen this delineation because there are significant differences in children of each group, both developmentally and psychologically. Certain techniques may work for one group and not another. This also will provide the practitioner with a broader spectrum of options depending on the age of the children that he or she serves. I also want to remind the reader to consider the fact that when working with young people on the autism spectrum, the emotional age of the child or adolescent must be considered. For example, an adolescent whose physical age is thirteen may be ill suited for a group of young adolescents because her emotional age is around age ten. I recommend careful screening and assessing the emotional age of the young person prior to adding them to a group.

Regarding the structure of the chapters, I have chosen to address the main issues that represent challenges for children on the autism spectrum and for which group therapy is most helpful. Each issue has a corresponding application of group therapy and a rationale for the technique or approach. My goal in doing so is to provide the professional with a series of easy to understand techniques and applications for specific problems related to children on the autism spectrum, and to provide a useful manual to those who want to implement group therapy for the young people with whom they work. The main areas that I will cover in this chapter are: 1) Emotional (dealing with frustration, understanding emotions, putting thoughts and feelings into words, and increasing emotional control); 2) Self-Awareness (learning perspective-taking, identity formation—"Who Am I?"—and instillation of self-worth); 3) Relational Skill Building (building friendships, learning how to get along with others, working together with others in a group, how to stand up for oneself—bullying prevention).

GROUP THERAPY APPLIED TO EMOTIONAL ISSUES OF YOUNGER CHILDREN ON THE AUTISM SPECTRUM

Children on the autism spectrum struggle with emotional problems. Some of the common issues include an inability to tolerate frustration or becoming easily frustrated, a lack of understanding of emotions and interpreting the emotions of others (alexithymia), and maintaining emotional control. Due to the intense nature of children on the autism spectrum, emotional difficulties are common. Emotional problems create many challenges in many areas for children, from forming and maintaining relationships to doing well academically. Children who cannot achieve emotional control are often shunned by peers because peers view them as unpredictable and immature. Many children on the autism spectrum display emotional intensity, meaning the child rarely is in the middle of the emotional spectrum. Instead, he or she is either riding the high of positive emotions, or is completely incapacitated and overwhelmed by negative emotions. Thus, even when the child is engaged in an activity she enjoys, the excitement can overwhelm her, resulting in impulsive behavior that brings negative choices and consequences.

The group therapy experience can be a wonderful place to learn about emotions, learn to manage emotions, and meet other individuals that also struggle with emotional problems. One of the joys I have experienced in my group work is seeing the reassuring shock in young people that realize there are other people in the world that feel like them, and who have struggles much like they do. A common issue for children on the autism spectrum who struggle with understanding emotions and maintaining emotional control is the consequences that result from impulsive behavior. The impact of this on the child is rejection from peers and constantly feeling "in trouble" at school and at home. The group therapy experience can give these children a sense of hope through camaraderie with others that share the same experience. I remember clearly one young man who sheepishly began to share with the group how he would bite himself when he got angry. He was surprised as the other boys showed him their bite marks, gouges on their legs where they scratched themselves, and bald patches where they pulled their hair out when they became frustrated. The boy's embarrassment immediately shifted to empowerment as he realized he was not alone in being overwhelmed by emotions and he was also very "normal" for physically releasing the overwhelming emotions that often consumed him.

First Order of Business: Setting of Group Rules

The first thing I recommend a therapist do who is attempting group therapy with children on the autism spectrum is to create a simple set of rules. Without them, and trust me when I say I've learned this the hard way, you are starting off in a haphazard direction. Children have a natural tendency to roam and explore their environment in a free manner. This is not because they are bad or "up to no good," but because a child, especially a young child, tends to see new places as sort of "theirs" to do what they want. Children on the spectrum can be a mix of both, freely taking off and exploring, or being reserved and very cautious, almost paralyzed at times when encountering a new environment. The rules help guide the group and give the child a clear set of expectations that help to shape behavior as well as quell possible anxiety. For children on the spectrum, as well as human beings in general, safety is one of our utmost needs. Rules and procedures help human beings feel safe. When people know and understand what is expected of them and what the parameters of behavior are, a state of chaos is avoided. Group rules should be tailored for both the age and ability of the group with whom you are working. Examples of rules that can be helpful are as follows:

1. Only one person talks at a time;
2. Keep hands and feet to yourself;
3. Raise your hand if you have something to say;
4. No mean words!

The therapist can also ask the group if they would like to add any rules. This can help instill a sense of safety in the members as well as self-confidence. Writing them down on a piece of poster board that can be easily brought out at the beginning of each group is very helpful to remind the group of what is expected.

The Colors of Emotions—What are Emotions?

This group therapy technique is designed to help younger children on the autism spectrum learn about what emotions are and to give them a picture of emotions through visualizing emotions as colors. This technique involves using colored paper where each color symbolizes a different emotion. For example, red may be used to symbolize anger, or being "really mad." Orange symbolizes frustration, yellow stands for "being annoyed," blue represents sadness or being "down," and green represents being happy, content, and in a calm state. The group leader can hold up one of the colors, such as red, and have each member talk about his or her experience when in that emotional state. This technique provides a foundation for later work in which the group members will learn techniques to self-soothe and deal with the emotional states. The therapist can take the technique one step further depending on the ability of the group by having the members write on the back or drawing a picture of being in that emotional state. Two positive things that come from this are that the members can realize that others struggle with controlling and understanding emotions, and the group members can practice putting thoughts into words and sharing those in a group experience. Thus, a valuable social skill is being taught and modeled while working on the emotional issues. This "killing two birds with one stone" phenomenon in which social skills work accompanies the technique of another issue such as emotions or perspective-taking will be evident throughout the book.

From Colors to Coping

The next step in using this technique is to begin to teach emotional coping skills to group members that go along with the negative emotions of anger and frustration. For example, the therapist can use the information that the group members have shared on one side of the colored paper and use the other side to write coping skills and techniques to combat the negative emotions. I like to give the children of the group some time to brainstorm some techniques to deal with negative emotions to ascertain the level of the knowledge of the group. Some children diagnosed with ASD have a good deal of knowledge about coping with negative emotions, especially those that have received services from a young age. Once the therapist has given the members one or two coping skills and written them on the paper, the members are given the chance to talk about a time when they *felt* like losing control but worked through the situation without an emotional or behavioral meltdown. I find that even the most emotionally volatile child can come up with at least one instance of where he or she demonstrated control when feeling a negative emotion. Sharing this information can be a self-worth booster for the child sharing the information as well as a learning opportunity for the other group members.

"I Don't Have to Freak Out!"

Sharon, a licensed therapist was leading a group of three boys diagnosed with ASD. John, Michael, and Timothy had all identified various situations in which they had experienced emotions and had written those on the corresponding pieces of paper. John drew a dinosaur-like monster on the back of his red piece of paper and stated, "When I get really mad I think I'm a monster, like a T-Rex." Timothy said he liked John's monster and showed the group how he had drawn a dragon on the back of his red paper. He told the group how he had been sent home from school because he had gotten so angry he tipped over a book shelf. He said that if he had been a dragon "fire would have come out of my mouth." Sharon praised both boys for sharing and began to talk about what someone can do when they feel angry. Michael raised his hand and said he had learned to ball up his fists and squeeze really tight when he felt angry. He said that when he let his fists open up, it felt like the anger was draining away and he said "I don't have to freak out!" The other boys laughed and repeated what Michael said. Sharon led the group in practicing Michael's technique and also added a few others such as counting, taking deep breaths, and doing push-ups. Each boy wrote these on the back of their red papers as well as the words, "I don't have to freak out!" The group then moved on to their yellow papers and the topic of frustration and annoyance and found coping skills for those as well. In the weeks following, the boys all had positive stories to tell about how they didn't "freak out" when they felt angry, frustrated, or annoyed.

Emotional Coping Skills—A Balloon Game to Teach Breathing Techniques

This technique is used to give each child a valuable coping skill when experiencing a negative emotion such as anger or frustration. One of the negative results of the activation of the sympathetic nervous system ("Fight or Flight") is the tendency to take short, shallow breaths and deplete the amount of oxygen that is sent to the brain. This technique helps young people learn how deep, even breathing can help the body and brain stay calm, and involves having fun at the same time. The activity begins with the therapist explaining the importance of breathing and how good breathing is useful in controlling anger. The therapist distributes a balloon to each group member and instructs him or her to think of something that "triggers" them and creates anger or frustration. Then each member is instructed to blow up his or her balloon. Once blown up, the therapist instructs each child to release the air out of the balloon and do it again. At this point, usually the group members are red-faced and huffing and puffing quite vigorously. The therapist can then ask each member, "What happened to your anger? Where did it go?" Usually, this exercise creates laughter and smiles and I stop the exercise at that point and get the group to focus on the feeling of happiness and safety that triggers the laughter and smiles. This part can be a connecting exercise to positive emotions and how a simple technique such as breathing and blowing up the balloon triggered a pleasant response. I have had some children who, after playing this game during group therapy, keep a balloon on hand at home to help them deal with anger and frustration, and some have even taught their parents the technique!

Board Games that Help Learn How to Deal with Frustration

Board games are a wonderful tool to use in group therapy, not only to teach the basic social skills of turn taking and following group rules, but the games can also help children learn to deal with negative emotions such as anger, frustration, and disappointment. Because younger children tend to have shorter attention spans, I like to use games that are fairly quick and easy to play. Some that I have used include: Operation, Trouble, Hungry Hippos, and Candy Land. I began incorporating board games into my group work after several parents told me how their young person diagnosed with ASD would not even attempt to play games at home because of being unable to tolerate the disappointment of losing and needing to "win at all costs." Board games also promote communication between members and allow for modeling and practice of social interaction around a specific event. Children diagnosed with ASD tend to like organized systems that rule based games provide, but many struggle to "like" something with which they are not familiar. I have found that an added benefit of using board games, especially those that the child is not familiar, puts the child in an unfamiliar situation in which they must learn something new. For many children diagnosed with ASD, learning a new skill or being in an unfamiliar situation creates frustration and anxiety. Playing a new game gives an opportunity for the child to experience aroused emotions but to push through them based on the fun activity and support of the group. This positive experience can give the child confidence as well as practice not being paralyzed by negative emotions.

Operation: From Frustration to Joy!

John, Michael, Julie, and Morgan gather around the game *Operation* and get the cards set up while the therapist makes sure all the pieces are in the proper places. John announces that he is going to "test" the buzzer and places the metal part of the tweezers on the metal on the side of the opening for the wishbone. The nose of the "patient" lights up and the familiar buzzing sounds in the room, and John lets out a happy squeal. Julie and Michael clap their hands in excitement and both say how excited they feel to play the game. The therapist notices that Morgan sits quietly, with a worried look on his face. When the therapist inquires as to what is wrong with Morgan, Morgan shares that games like *Operation* are not fun because "I always fail, and it makes me frustrated when I fail." The therapist tells Morgan that he doesn't have to play, he can just watch the others and if he wants to join in later he can. Morgan nods his head and says "Okay." The game begins and John, Michael, and Julie all take turns. Each one lets out cries of joy and disappointment as a piece is successfully recovered, and as the buzzer sounds as the side of the cavity is touched. Julie turns to Morgan and begs him to join the game. Reluctantly, he agrees but loudly announces that he is *not* going to try Writer's Cramp! He draws a card called "Spare Ribs" and the others encourage him as he tentatively attempts to retrieve the piece. Morgan tells the others, "Stop! You're making me nervous!" and they become quiet as they follow his stern command. Everyone watches as Morgan reaches in and grabs the spare ribs and pulls out the tweezers. He seems more surprised than anyone else and lets out a whoop of joy as he holds up the tweezers. "I did it!" Morgan exclaims. The others clap and tell Morgan "Good job!" as they decide whose turn it is. The group persuades Morgan to try getting another piece and this time the buzzer goes off. He instantly slouches while he drops the tweezers and hangs his head. The others encourage him and take their turns. The therapist notices that while Morgan is disappointed, he does not leave the group or lose emotional control. Suddenly, it is his turn again and reluctantly, he draws a card. This time, he extracts the piece and again shows great enthusiasm as the others are again excited for him. The game goes on. Twice more Morgan does not get his piece and sets off the light and the buzzer, but each time he is less disappointed. By the end of the game he remarks to the therapist, "It's okay to try something even if you don't get it right every time. I think I like *Operation* now."

Group Sand Play

Sand is a powerful tool in the world of play therapy (Hull, 2011; Norton & Norton, 1997; Richardson, 2012). The sand tray becomes a world that the individual is free to explore and create representations of his or her internal events and experiences. Sand play can be used in the group therapy forum and I have found that it is very useful with children of all ages, as well as adolescents and even adults. Using the sand tray in the group therapy format has the following benefits for young people on the autism spectrum. First, group sand play is an opportunity for group members to join in an activity together. This promotes a sense of togetherness that models real-world scenarios that teaches working in groups. This will benefit the young people as they get older, as many of the tasks of adolescence and adulthood require a person to be able to work in a group setting with other people. Second, group sand play is an opportunity for group members to create and explore in the group setting. This can help the young person learn to express themselves in a group atmosphere and build up his or her sense of self-confidence. Many young people on the autism spectrum become paralyzed by fear in group settings and struggle with self-expression, even though deep down there is a desire to do so. A third reason why group sand play is useful is it offers an opportunity for the young person to learn to communicate with others, not only about what is being created, but what the young person is experiencing emotionally.

I use two different approaches using sand play in the group setting. The first is assigning a task that must be completed, such as building a mountain and making a tunnel through the middle (this requires wet sand that can be molded and shaped) or creating a city or town. Each child is assigned a certain task and they must work together. A "foreman" can be used, depending on the dynamics of the group in which one of the children is voted to be the overseer of the project. This position can be rotated so that each child practices the leadership role and learns to follow the leadership of a peer. Changes or modifications must be voted on, and requests must be clearly communicated. This approach demands that the therapist stay on top of each child's involvement and be ready to monitor for a child who is not involved, or is trying to "take over." The benefits of this approach include learning to take direction from a peer, learning to be in a leadership role (especially for the more passive and shy individuals), and learning to work together to create something that is one unit built of many individual parts. Another variation of this approach is the group creates a story through the sand play. For instance, one child is the "director" and appoints the other members to use characters (such as LEGO® mini-figures) and other materials (such as a castle) to tell a story. This also teaches group interaction as well as individual expression and following the lead of a peer. The "director" role can be rotated and each "story" can be given a time limit (ten minutes, etc.) so that each member gets a turn. These stories can be videotaped and watched by the group members which can help teach perspective-taking.

The second approach of using sand play in group therapy is simply a free play activity in which the children are free to take a corner of the sand tray and create whatever they choose. A box of toys that can be used in the sand tray is placed nearby and the group members are free to use those or simply create something from the sand itself. I have found that some children on the autism spectrum are sometimes hesitant to play with sand. Some do not like sand because of the way it feels on their hands or it may remind them of being dirty, and some have a fear of bugs or worms and do not believe the sand is washed and clean. The free play activity is a good way to introduce the sand tray and find out if there is a group member with an aversion to sand, and also to get the children familiar with the sand tray.

The Great Castle in the Sand

One of the groups I conduct loves to create stories that involve the sand tray. This play began as free exploration of the sand tray and then shifted to a more directive form of sand play as I explained in the earlier section. Each member of the group struggles with fear and low self-confidence, and the sand play has been a way for each member to conquer fear. The play centers on a castle that is placed in the sand tray and each member chooses a LEGO® mini-figure that represents him or her. Before play begins, each group member explains the characteristics of their character and why he or she was chosen. This element has helped me teach self-awareness as well as helping the members understand personality differences and recognizing differences in others. At each group meeting, a different member gets a turn at being the "director" and sets the stage for what is going to happen during that day's meeting. The other members can modify the story but must check in with the director first. When too many ideas begin flying at once, I encourage the director to say "Cut!" or "Time out!" in order to restore a sense of order in the story-building phase. This helps to instill self-confidence in the member playing the "director" by demonstrating assertive behavior as I mentioned above.

The characters are explained and the story is set. Usually, there is a set of "bad" people that are trying to take over the castle or steal something within the castle, and the group works together to defeat the "bad" people and defend the castle. The castle represents a wonderful metaphor of a person or group; the "defense" of the castle can be taught as valuing a person's self or being, or being a part of a close group that has one common goal. This group has labeled the sand play the "Great Castle in the Sand," and sometimes the play is recorded to be watched later, much like how athletes spend time after a game watching "film." The group members enjoy seeing themselves on camera and I use that time to pause the recording and point out to each one how he or she overcame fear as well as discussing communication styles and teaching how to shift from the play to real-life scenarios in which the children can put into practice what has been played out. This technique demonstrates the effectiveness of group sand play and how various skills can be taught and learned through a fun activity.

Group LEGO®Play

Many authors have cited the usefulness of LEGO® in working with children and adolescents on the autism spectrum (Hull, 2012; LeGoff, 2004, 2006; Owens, Granader, Humphrey, & Baron-Cohen, 2008). The draw to LEGO® for individuals on the spectrum is "due to the fact that people with autism are particularly attracted to systems" (Owens, et al., p. 1945). LeGoff (2004) discusses the various elements of group LEGO® play which involves getting a group of children to work together towards a common goal. This is not only fun and involves a system of play that children are familiar with, but also is a method to teach social and emotional skill building. Group LEGO® play helps increase joint attention, communication, problem solving, and conflict resolution skills (LeGoff, 2004, 2006). I continue to be amazed at how children diagnosed with ASD enjoy LEGO® and how many useful applications LEGO® provides in both individual and group therapy sessions. Much like the group sand play, I use group LEGO® play in two ways: structured, organized play and unstructured free play.

The structured, organized group LEGO® play follows the same format LeGoff (2004) described in that the children are given a task that involves building a LEGO® structure. An "engineer" directs the building project, while "builders" set about working together to create the structure (LeGoff, 2004). Through this type of task, group members must work together by using individual effort that is directed towards a group goal. Along the way, communication, joint attention, social skills, and recognition of non-verbal cues are practiced. I have used these types of groups for years and one great benefit I have noticed is the improvement in self-worth and confidence level of the children who partake in the group LEGO® play. Many children diagnosed with ASD struggle with low self-worth, have a lack of self-confidence, and appear almost paralyzed by fear when faced with speaking in a group. Having a safe place like the group therapy environment surrounded by peers that struggle with the same issues and being involved in LEGO® play can give a child a sense of safety that translates into confidence. I have witnessed many quiet and shy young people gradually become assertive and confident as they take on the role of the engineer and direct the builders. LeGoff (2004) also discusses allowing the group members to work in pairs, using an "engineer" and a "builder," each taking turns after a set amount of time. I have used this format often, especially with extremely shy or lower functioning individuals diagnosed with ASD as a way to gradually get them warmed up to the idea of participating in a larger group.

The second way that group LEGO® play can be used is in unstructured free play format. Similar to the experience I discussed in the group sand play section, the members are free to sift through the building materials and explore. I have found this is helpful to orient children if they are unfamiliar with LEGO®, as well as a way to assess the social skill level of group members by observing which members connect with another member, who, if any, will ask for help, and if any negative behaviors emerge from a member during this time. Some children diagnosed with ASD are very rigid and work hard to be in control at all times, which is related to safety as I explained earlier in the book. I have encountered children diagnosed with ASD that have never engaged in group play, and many have no siblings. These children sometimes experience a mixture of shock and horror that another child might want to use a piece of LEGO®, not as a part of the "Death Star" from Star Wars as the piece was initially intended, but instead as an umbrella for their LEGO® horses in a pasture. You can imagine how hard it can be for a child diagnosed with ASD who is very rigid and inflexible to adapt to such conditions, and yet, also very necessary as he or she moves towards adolescence and one day, adulthood. I recall one young boy who had no siblings and whose every whim and obsession was indulged by parents who were just trying to do their best; he actually became so upset in group that he had to be removed. We decided that he was not ready for group yet, but continued working together in individual therapy. Eventually, he was gradually introduced back into the group experience and slowly but surely made significant gains in the area of social skills and adapting to the group environment. The use of LEGO® in the unstructured free play format can help the therapist discern these types of issues in group members.

LEGO® Mini-Figures

Since I am discussing the topic of LEGO®, I also want to discuss the use of LEGO® mini-figures. The LEGO® mini-figure has been an invaluable tool in my work with young people for teaching social skills, and helping to explain personality, as well as character development for children diagnosed with ASD. There are literally thousands of mini-figures, each with individual expressions and characteristics. While many are characters represented in movies and TV shows, many are simply representations of everyday people children see around them. One way I use the mini-figures is in the technique I described when discussing group sand play. Each group member is allowed to pick a figure that represents who he or she would like to "be" and then the group member guides their mini-figure through the play and uses their figure to interact with other group members' mini-figures. The group member takes on the voice and mannerisms of their character and in doing so is able to experiment with aspects of a different persona or self that is different from how he or she usually is. I have used this type of play in which a child emulates a character whether through doll play, puppet play, or with LEGO® mini-figures, as a way to "push" the child into a sort of self-experimentation. Because individuals diagnosed with ASD often do not engage in pretend play, many have not experienced the satisfaction of pretending to be another person. Thus, because much of our adaptation in social settings and gaining maturity comes from imitating the behavior we see in others, many individuals diagnosed with ASD miss these important social cues and stay "stuck" and appear to be immature and obstinate. Using LEGO® mini-figures in play can help the young person begin to experiment with other roles and also help improve his or her perspective-taking ability.

"If Indy Can Do It, Then So Can I!"

Fear is a common element in the human experience in general, but fear is particularly problematic for individuals diagnosed with ASD. John, about ten years old, was part of one of my groups and he suffered from many fears. Some of John's fears were related to weather and natural disasters, but there was also a strong aversion to any new person or situation because the boy felt afraid if he was not in total control. I was seeing John in individual therapy and his parents wanted to include him in the group therapy sessions to help with socialization as well as working on his emotional issues in a group setting. John loved LEGO® and one character that he really enjoyed was Indiana Jones. During our individual sessions, John told me all about his love of Indiana Jones and we dissected the underlying character traits of bravery, intelligence, and calculated risk-taking behavior that “Indy” displayed repeatedly. We often played LEGO® Indiana Jones and John would marvel at Indy’s skills and he liked the determined look on the character’s face on the box of the game.

When John joined the group, he was thrilled to see how the group used LEGO® figures and he instantly created an Indiana Jones character and I allowed John to share with the group all about his hero. One day, we were talking about fear and I had the group members pretend they were approaching that fear as their character with the character’s intellect and skills. One boy whose favorite character was a Navy Seal, talked about how he was no longer afraid of being home alone because he had survival skills and weapons that kept him safe (positive thinking and getting rid of fear) just like a Navy Seal had weapons and skills that kept him safe. Each group member shared a similar metaphor between themselves and their chosen character. While John waited his turn, I noticed as he listened to the others that he became very excited and restless; he squirmed and shifted in his seat on the floor and put his hand up repeatedly as if he was going to burst. Finally, I called on him and he could contain himself no longer. Holding up his minifigure he shouted, “Indiana Jones isn’t afraid of anything, and I don’t have to be afraid either!” and then went on. “Well, he actually was afraid of snakes but I’m actually not afraid of them, so that’s one thing, but I can be brave like him. If Indy can do it, then so can I!” The others nodded in agreement, and all of us in the room that day were inspired by John’s speech. It was one more step in John’s life of trying new things and meeting new people, and realizing that he did not have to be afraid.

GROUP THERAPY APPLIED TO INCREASING PERSPECTIVE-TAKING FOR YOUNGER CHILDREN ON THE AUTISM SPECTRUM

I have discussed in earlier chapters how mindblindness, or the lack of perspective-taking is problematic for individuals diagnosed with ASD. Mindblindness is like living with tunnel vision or wearing blinders. Mindblindness contributes to the appearance of a lack of empathy and can negatively affect the individual’s ability to form relationships with others and function in social settings. For children in particular, mindblindness creates great difficulty in learning social cues that are part of building blocks for later development and advance social behavior. The group experience offers great opportunities to help young people learn to see things from a different perspective, and to at least introduce the concept. I have had the privilege of watching young people begin to gain better social skills as a result of group therapy, particularly in the area of perspective-taking. Group therapy is helpful in decreasing mindblindness in several ways. One is that the group environment offers the child a structured place to observe and interact with others. Large group settings such as schools can reinforce the characteristics of mindblindness in that the school environment can be overwhelming with noise and large numbers of people. Children on the spectrum can often retreat into the safety of hiding deep within themselves, despite the fact that he or she is surrounded by many individuals. The group environment contains less people, is usually quiet and comfortable, and is a fun and familiar place that creates a space to learn and grow.

A second reason that group therapy is helpful in reducing mindblindness is that the group therapy environment can introduce skills gradually, which helps to reduce feelings of being bombarded or overwhelmed. I have found that many social skills training programs introduce a lot of concepts without realizing that time is key in how a child, especially one on the autism spectrum, is able to absorb the information. Most children are emotionally immature and because they are in various stages of brain development, there is only so much information that can be absorbed at any given time. The group therapy environment offers the opportunity for a consistent stream of skill teaching that can be done at a moderate pace that takes into account the challenges of ASD as well as the individual characteristics of the child.

A third and final reason why group therapy with children diagnosed with ASD is effective in reducing mindblindness is the connection with others in the group experience. The small group, made up of just a few peers not only helps to reduce the natural fear and apprehension that children on the autism spectrum often feel in social settings, but also offers the opportunity to meet comrades to emulate. Often, children feel empowered in simply knowing that other young people struggle with the same fears and social challenges that they face. I have witnessed the increase in perspective-taking during group therapy when these fears and challenges are shared, and a child realizes that he or she is not "the only one." One boy in particular sat open-mouthed as he heard another boy share about the bully that constantly antagonized him at school. This young man had always thought that he was "the only one" who had problems with bullies. Despite the fact that teachers and his parents had told him that others had the same problem, he could not see it until he heard it from a peer. I have witnessed this same phenomenon related to problems with bullies and bed-wetting, as well as struggles with siblings and thoughts of suicide. The ability to see things from another perspective gives all of us a sense of empowerment and strength to move through a problem; when one knows that others are struggling through the same issue there is a strengthening of resolve.

The following techniques are designed to help younger children diagnosed with ASD learn to take a different perspective.

Follow the Leader

A very simple game that is a fun way to introduce perspective-taking with children diagnosed with ASD in group therapy is "Follow the Leader." Schmidt and Heybyrne (2004) discuss the use of "Follow the Leader" as a way to get children diagnosed with ASD to notice peers and to pattern the behavior of others. Each group member is allowed to play the "leader" role and the therapist keeps time to make sure that each member gets a turn. The game can be varied by giving the leaders a specific task to complete that all group members must repeat, or the leaders can be given freedom to do as they wish. The therapist monitors for those who are not watching the leader or not following the leader's movements and gestures. This game is fun and creates great excitement. I find that the game also helps develop a sense of self-worth in the member who is playing the "leader" as they realize that they are "in charge" and it is a wondrous sight to see a child realize that others are watching and following his or her every move. The members who are following the leader work hard to mimic every move and in doing so practice watching another's movements, facial expressions, and voice tones and inflections. Following the game, the therapist can sit with the group members and process members' thoughts and feelings and reinforce the concept of perspective-taking.

The PEZ Game

I wrote about "The PEZ Game" in my first book and explained how it is a fun and useful way to help increase perspective-taking in children (Hull, 2011). I stumbled upon this technique quite by accident. One day a boy diagnosed with ASD was standing by my collection of PEZ dispensers and seemed to be talking to himself. As I moved closer to observe him, I noticed that he was playing with the Winnie the Pooh set that someone had given me. Because he loved Winnie the Pooh, he was drawn to the characters and I was surprised to hear him imitating the voices of Pooh, Piglet, Eeyore, Rabbit, and Kangaroo. I invited him to bring the PEZ dispensers to the middle of the room and show me what was happening. He picked them up and brought them down on the floor. As he played, I was able to ask him questions, such as "What is Pooh thinking now?" and "What do you think Eeyore is feeling?" We began to play out scenarios with the PEZ dispensers and I noticed that the boy gradually started to show an improvement in perspective-taking in various settings like home and at school, and his mother told me that she noticed an increase in his displays of empathy and helping behavior around the house.

The technique with the young man got me thinking to try using PEZ dispensers in my group therapy sessions. If you choose to fill the dispensers with candy be careful to check with parents to make sure that their child can eat the candy (the first young man I referenced above was on a strict diet so I made sure that there was no candy in the dispensers when he came for his sessions). Each member of the group is allowed to choose a character that he or she likes, and if the therapist wishes each child can say why he or she chose their specific character. Much like the technique with the LEGO® mini-figures, each child plays the character that he or she has chosen within the group. However, after a few minutes of play the therapist stops play and each member must say what his character is thinking and feeling and then must pick another character and identify what he or she thinks that character might be thinking and feeling as well. If a member can answer these questions, he or she is allowed to take a piece of candy from their dispenser. For example, one of the groups that I conduct happens to have members who all love superheroes. I have several superhero PEZ dispensers and the group creates a story and all the members join in using their characters and joining in the stories. I will allow the play to go for a few minutes and then I will call out "FREEZE!" and the story stops. At this point I will ask the boy who is holding the Incredible Hulk what he thinks his character is feeling and thinking. I will then ask the boy holding the Incredible Hulk to tell the group what he thinks Spiderman is thinking and feeling, and so on. I try to not take up too much time and sometimes I may just ask one member per break of play. At the end of the group time, I will emphasize the various thoughts and feelings that were mentioned during group in order to reinforce how each member was able to identify what another character was thinking and feeling. The goal of this technique is to get each child to gain awareness into the thoughts and feelings of others through using characters that he or she identifies with and in a fun way.

Video/Computer Games in Group Therapy

My doctoral dissertation examined the use of video/computer games as a play therapy tool in working with children/adolescents suffering from emotional disturbances (Hull, 2009) and it reminded me of how useful video/computer games are in the therapy process. Since that time I have used video/computer games in group therapy and have found that using the games in the group therapy format is very useful, particularly to help with teaching perspective-taking. One useful element of using the games in the group therapy environment is that group members must take turns. Taking turns is a common part of any social interaction and is a foundation of our culture. Everywhere one looks in American culture, there is the phenomenon of standing in line and waiting one's turn—from the water fountain line to placing one's order at a fast-food restaurant. Children in general, especially young children, have to be taught this important foundational brick of social strata, and children diagnosed with ASD sometimes struggle with this concept due to mindblindness. Through a fun activity like waiting one's turn to play a video/

computer game, children can be taught this important concept. A second way that video/computer games are useful in increasing perspective-taking is that the games give the young person the opportunity to play a character who is facing challenges, creating parts of a world, or interacting with other characters within the game. Games can be paused and discussion can take place regarding what a character may be thinking or feeling. Online gaming through a computer game such as MineCraft links players and creates the opportunity for social connections that allow the therapist to not only teach social skills, but also to get the young person to imagine what another player is thinking or feeling.

Mario Bros. Group Therapy!

I have a Nintendo Entertainment System (NES) at my office and I have several of the Mario Bros. games. Most children are familiar with Mario Bros. and I have used the games for many years in individual therapy and have discovered metaphors that relate to helping children, adolescents, and adults gain coping skills. One obvious metaphor that the games provide is overcoming challenges and facing obstacles that block the path to success. A player must beat "Goombas," face ghosts and "Thwomps," as well as beating the "boss" at the end of each level. These obstacles in the game can take the form of the bullies, school work, and tough decisions that people must face each day. For my group, I set up four chairs in front of the TV and game system. The members roll dice to see who will go first. I put the game on two-player mode and then it is decided how the players will take turns. Each player takes a turn and does their best to get through the level. I have formulated some rules that are helpful to provide structure during video game group play. One is that no one may make fun of another player's "failure;" encouragement is a must. Also, there is to be no grabbing or snatching the controller out of another player's hands. Third and last, there is to be no shouting or tantrums if a player does not succeed. If a group member becomes excessively distressed, he or she may remove themselves. I also use group video game play to learn to manage negative emotions such as anger, disappointment, and frustration. I will discuss this in the next chapter related to older children and adolescents.

During the game play, I will randomly press the pause button on the game controller so that group discussion can be used related to practicing perspective-taking. For example, assume that Christopher just completed a very difficult level. I may ask Christopher what he was feeling and thinking as he worked through the level, and also some of the emotions that he felt at the end of the completion of the level. Then I will call on another member to repeat back what Christopher said so that each member can begin to imagine being in Christopher's shoes. As each player plays, the game action is paused so that this interaction can happen. The goal is that through the similar experience of the game play, each member can begin to identify with another player's thoughts and feelings based on the similarities of his or her own game play experience. The therapist can also conclude the group session with a summary of the experience of being in "another's shoes" and what it was like to hear others' thoughts and feelings when doing the same activity.

Story Telling and Role Play

This technique not only helps to begin instilling perspective-taking skills, but also is helpful in building up self-worth and confidence through the experience of telling a story to a group. I find that many young people on the autism spectrum have quite a lot to say, but rarely do they get to address a captive audience. This is yet another indirect benefit of the group experience for individuals diagnosed with ASD. This technique also teaches the social skill of turn-taking which always involves learning patience and reinforces the need to wait on others and speak at an appropriate time. The group members decide who will go first and it is important for the therapist to explain the importance of careful listening to the storyteller. This also helps work on the skill of joint attention and focused attention by group members. I recommend that the storyteller be given a time limit through the use of a timer which the storyteller can be aware of also to keep him or her "on track." Many children diagnosed with ASD do poorly with keeping track of time, especially when it involves an activity that relates to something that they find interesting. I usually give group members between three and five minutes to tell their story. This limited time also helps keep the group members' attention and keeps the details of the story to a minimum, which makes it easier for group members to follow. Following the story, the group is organized to act out parts of the story. For example, one group member takes the point of view of the storyteller and the other members become other characters that are a part of the story. The acting out of the story helps reinforce for the group members the importance of listening to the details of others' stories and then to identify thoughts and feelings embedded in the story. I limit the acting out of the story to between five and ten minutes. The main elements that need to be emphasized are the group members being able to identify the point of view of the storyteller through connecting with the thoughts and feelings that were expressed. At the end of the group session, it is helpful for the therapist to highlight the fundamentals of perspective-taking and to allow what was practiced to "sink in."

Thought Bubbles: What Are They Thinking?

Thought-bubble training with children on the autism spectrum has been discussed in the literature for some time (Wellman, Baron-Cohen, Caswell,

Gomez, Swettenham, Toye, & Lagattuta, 2002). While the results of the training are controversial, many find that using thought bubbles does help teach ToM and increase perspective-taking in individuals diagnosed with ASD (Paynter & Peterson, 2013). The use of thought bubbles in training young people diagnosed with ASD have produced mixed results, but I have found them to be a helpful tool in both individual and group therapy work. I encourage each therapist to dig into the literature and read the findings, but I also want to stress the importance of imagination and freedom to explore the approaches that are written about in order to help those on the autism spectrum. The autism spectrum is too vast and the individual characteristics of the amazing people on that spectrum are too immense to think that a technique that did not "generalize" to a large population is one that should be discarded. We never know what technique or part of a technique may play a vital role in the development of a valuable skill for an individual diagnosed with ASD. I am constantly reminded of this when I think of John Elder Robinson's journey of learning to interpret others' behavior and teach himself social skills (Robinson, 2007).

I have used thought-bubble training in group therapy with young people and I believe that it helps to introduce the concept of perspective-taking with younger children, and to reinforce the concept with older children and adolescents. In my quest to keep techniques simple and as affordable as possible, I use a large piece of drawing paper and a marker, on which I draw stick people in random situations with an empty thought bubble above the character's head. I also use a white board which has the added advantage of quickly changing a character's facial expression or adding other people in the scene. My use of thought-bubble training has an extra "twist" that I use in that I take the real-world issues that the individual group members have shared and incorporate them into the thought-bubble scenarios. For example, Richard has a difficult time getting along with his two sisters who happen to be younger than he. He is constantly getting in trouble because of his emotional reaction to his sister's behaviors, who love to push his "buttons" and watch him melt down emotionally. Richard has identified this problem as "the biggest problem of my life, bigger than World War II." Using thought bubbles, I draw Richard and then his sisters. Leaving the thought bubbles empty, the group as well as Richard walk through a scenario that he has described and the group members try to come up with what they think the sisters and Richard may be thinking. This helps to instill skills of ignoring another person's negative behavior and finding coping skills instead of reacting in a negative emotional manner. I have witnessed the phenomenon of a light bulb going off in young people's heads as he or she realizes that reacting negatively was their only option. However, due to the thought-bubble training, he or she could see a ray of hope because they could understand the situation from another angle. This technique can also be modified to practice the "socially acceptable response." For example, Henry gets annoyed when his parents demand that he answer them in complete sentences and to use words instead of shrugs or grunts. Using thought bubbles and dialogue bubbles, Henry can write in what he is supposed to say and even though it annoys him, I can write in a positive thought that his mother is thinking when he responds appropriately. I have seen this exercise help young people pull out of a selfish mind-set and many begin to demonstrate empathy as a result of increased perspective-taking. I also use the thought-bubble technique as a way to introduce concepts from Cognitive Therapy as well as Rational Emotive Behavioral Therapy (REBT) by showing how the character's facial expressions will change to reveal different emotional states when the thoughts of the character are shifted from negative and irrational to positive and rational.

GROUP THERAPY APPLIED TO INCREASING SELF-WORTH AND SELF-AWARENESS FOR YOUNGER CHILDREN ON THE AUTISM SPECTRUM

Children diagnosed with ASD often have a sense of low self-worth (Hull, 2011). Many experience low self-worth because of environmental factors like peer rejection or bullying (Carter, 2009). I find that many are very tender-hearted and get their feelings hurt very easily. Sometimes this is due to emotional immaturity and the inability to interpret the emotions of others or understand their emotions. One significant finding that struck me is the way in which children diagnosed with ASD tend to blame themselves when encountering rejection from others and this causes negative thought patterns which follow them through developmental stages and into the adult years (Baron-Cohen, 2000). It appears that these "neural pathways" can become rigid and fixed; early intervention in the form of individual and group therapy can be very helpful to reverse this terrible cycle. Children diagnosed with ASD are at higher risk for suffering from low self-worth because of the complexity of issues that arise due to alexithymia, mindblindness, and the general feeling of being "lost" in a world that moves quickly and in confusing and unpredictable patterns. Part of the role of the therapist is to help instill a sense of self-worth in the child or adolescent so that he or she may take pride in who they are and what they do and find enjoyment and fulfillment in life. A healthy sense of self-worth is important also for instilling a sense of confidence that can translate into building healthy relationships and pursuing career goals.

Group therapy provides many benefits towards helping a young person diagnosed with ASD gain skills in developing a sense of self-worth. The dynamic that group therapy offers of finding others who struggle with the same issues creates a force of encouragement and strength. A second benefit is that a group setting can help to affirm the young person's gifts and talents which can help him or her see the value in who they are and that the young person has much to offer to the world around them. One of my joys in group therapy work is seeing the surprise on a young person's face when he or she realizes that the group members honestly value his or her opinion and the other members find meaning in what the young person can say or do. This "shock" helps to get the young person to begin to see themselves as valuable and worthy, and that there is a purpose and reason for him or her being on the planet. A third and final benefit is that the group therapy setting helps to strengthen the sense of self-worth through consistent affirmation and provides a safe place for the young person to continue to grow and learn.

A healthy sense of self-awareness is as important as a sense of self-worth. A person who is not self-aware will have difficulty navigating the social world and forming healthy attachments. Until a person gains a sense of self-awareness, attempting to build social skills will likely be a waste of time as there is no context for the skills if they cannot be aware of their actions. Group therapy can be useful in instilling a sense of self-awareness in a person diagnosed with ASD. The following techniques will focus on helping to instill a sense of self-worth and self-awareness in younger children diagnosed with ASD. I feel that I need to stress to the reader the need to remember the individuality of children diagnosed with ASD and that in the group setting, the group members will probably grasp concepts at different rates based on their level of ability and place on the autism spectrum. Be patient, be consistent, and keep a high level of encouragement and optimism.

Show and Tell

Do you remember the days of "Show and Tell" in school? Remember the good feeling that came from bringing in your favorite Matchbox car or Barbie doll? Remember how good it felt to show off something that you made or found? Talking about what we love and showing items to others seems to be an innate human need that spans cultural divides and geographical regions. Sadly, most schools have done away with show and tell. Curriculums of today have little time for this precious pastime that seems to be embedded in the human psyche. I have observed this phenomenon in many of the children with whom I have worked over the years as a girl or boy eagerly rushes into my office carrying their latest LEGO® creation or newest addition to their doll collection. A new pet is eagerly shown and talked about, whether it is a dog, turtle, or bird. Even adolescents are eager to show me a YouTube video posting, Facebook or Tumblr page, or show me their most recent art creations. I have found that this is universal in the young people with whom I work, whether neurotypical or on the autism spectrum. My experience in group therapy is no different, and I have found that allowing a time for show and tell can do wonders for helping to instill a child's sense of self-worth.

My approach is simple and straightforward. I use a timer and each member is given five minutes to share one item to talk about. Early on, I failed to give parameters and some children would bring nearly every possession he or she owned. As usual, we learn as we go. I found that by limiting it to one item, it reduced the pressure on the child and the experience could be richer as the group members also could direct their focus to the one item. There are a few minutes designated for discussion and with the child's permission, group members are allowed to touch or hold the item. Later on, we may even incorporate the item into the group play. Some interesting things that have been brought to group therapy that I recall are a feather collection, a bone collection, and a homemade windmill that actually created an electrical current.

The goal of the technique is that children are given the opportunity to talk about and show something that is meaningful to them, and that through the sharing, the sense of value and worth of the item or experience is transferred to the children. For example, Roger is very proud of a LEGO® creation that he built. It took him a long time and it was the first one that he did without any help from either of his parents. He brings his creation to group and the other members "ooh" and "ahh" over his creation and one of them blurts out, "I have that one but I couldn't do it by myself; my dad had to help me!" Roger beams as the other boys congratulate him on his work. He feels good—competent, smart, and admired by his peers. Through the object of his LEGO® creation, of which Roger is very proud, Roger becomes proud of himself as well. He is proud of his effort and the result of his effort. He realizes that he is good and good at something and this feeling stays with him. He begins to work harder at school, he works harder to please his mother at home, and also begins to keep his LEGO® pieces organized and his room neater because he suddenly realizes that he is valuable through the experience of building his creation and sharing it during group therapy.

Roger's positive experience is something that may stay with him for the rest of his life. This experience can definitely generalize to other parts of his life and help to raise his sense of self-worth as Roger finds value in who he is and as he becomes proud of the effort that he puts into various tasks. At the end of the show and tell session, I like to summarize the items shared and focus on the meaning of the item to each group member. Many times the group members will begin a discussion through asking each other questions about their particular item and why it means so much to them. Often, members will end up teaching the group a valuable skill through the experience. Overall, the goal of the experience is to give the group members an opportunity to share something that they love and that through doing so, the young people will have a greater sense of self-worth as a result.

I am Unique!

I discuss a technique called "I am Unique" in my book *Play Therapy and Asperger's* (Hull, 2011). This technique was originally designed for individual therapy work, but I have adapted it for group therapy work as well. The individual approach involves the therapist compiling a list of all the characteristics and interests of the child and the goal is to "help the child see the special interests and abilities that make up who they are, and to build a pathway to increasing self-worth" (Hull, 2011, p. 43). For the group approach I use a large piece of paper for each member. Using a marker, I draw a large stick figure that represents each child. Then, I have each child call out something that he or she likes or a personal characteristic that he or she likes while I write them on the paper around the figure. The group technique is modified to include the other members' input about a particular group member. For example, while Jennifer is telling me something she likes to do, Henry calls out and says that she is "nice and always helps me when I can't get through the level in Super Mario." I write that on the paper and also make sure to praise Henry for his compliment. At the end of this part of the exercise, I line up all the papers and each group member stands or sits by the paper that represents him or herself. Each member shares about their interests and characteristics that are written on the paper. Group members can ask questions or make comments about each others' attributes and interests and sometimes there is some nice dialogue that gets going between group members. Again, the main goal of this exercise is to promote a sense of value and worth as well as self-awareness in each group member.

Be the Teacher!

Many children diagnosed with ASD have specified interests that are a result of the child's laser-like focus and obsessive nature. Many have written about how the child's specified interest is a wonderful tool to use in the therapy process (Hull, 2011; LeGoff, 2004). I have incorporated the specified interests of children diagnosed with ASD into the group therapy process with the "Be the Teacher" technique that helps with building up a child's sense of self-worth. I introduce this technique after the group is established and after there is a good amount of familiarity and cohesion. As the group continues to meet, the specified interests of the members will gradually begin to surface, and I have found this happens quite quickly. I never want to embarrass a child or make them feel "put on the spot" so I ask them if they would be willing to, at the next group meeting, spend a few minutes teaching the group about their specified interest. I only allow one teaching session per group; otherwise, there would be chaos with each member vying for sufficient time to teach the group about his or her passion. I have learned much from these sessions, from learning to draw certain superheroes and creating origami animals, to playing various video games and reading previously unknown works of Japanese anime and comic books.

An Origami Lesson

Barry loved origami. Every group session involved him bringing a new creation. Usually, one or two group members would huddle with Barry after group to learn some technique of paper folding. The therapist asked Barry if he would like to teach the group an origami technique at the next group and if there was a simple creation that would only take a few minutes to teach and learn. Barry was pleased. He told the therapist that he knew the perfect creation. At the next group, the group was told that there was going to be an origami lesson taught by an origami master! The group was excited and then it was revealed that Barry would be the instructor. Barry beamed, obviously excited to share his passion for the ancient art of paper folding. Each group member was given a piece of paper that Barry brought and had cut to the exact dimension that was needed for the project. Barry walked the group through each step, carefully checking to make sure that each member was following along. A few of the members became frustrated during some of the steps and Barry was quick to help them. Soon, after about twenty minutes, each member had made a paper bird with moveable wings! The therapist praised Barry for his teaching ability and the patience that he displayed. The therapist also praised the group members for showing an interest and for pushing through the frustration that comes with learning something new. That day as the group was leaving, Barry remarked to the therapist, "You know, one day I might be a teacher or a college professor!" In later weeks, Barry's mother reported to the therapist how Barry had displayed a new level of self-confidence and had made new friends in the neighborhood, and that he had taught them all how to make an origami creation!

Pass the Ball!

This technique is a good way to start a group when members are getting acquainted or when a new member joins the group. This technique is multi-layered and contains elements of social skill-building in the form of speaking publicly and taking turns, as well as a way to build up a sense of self-worth and self-awareness. The group members sit on the floor forming a circle. The therapist takes the ball and begins by saying his or her name, and then shares something about him or herself or about a recent experience. The therapist then calls the name of a child in the group and passes the ball gently to the child. The child who receives the ball also says his or her name, shares some information, and then calls the name of the child that he or she wishes to pass the ball to and then passes the ball. This technique can be modified to include any topic that the therapist wishes to cover such as "Something that Scares

Me" or "What I Feel Like When I Get Bullied," and is a good way to get communication started between group members. This technique is a good way to introduce group conversation to children diagnosed with ASD to demonstrate how conversation "flows" and "bounces" along like the ball passing from person to person. The technique also helps to pull the child out of the isolative and solitary world that he or she is usually in, as well as offering them a way to say something that they find meaningful to a captive audience. This helps to instill a sense of self-worth and self-awareness.

Group Sand Play/Group LEGO® Play

Group sand play and group LEGO® play have much to offer in regards to raising a young person's sense of self-worth and self-awareness. One benefit of group sand and LEGO® play is that the child can take on a persona of a character through play that represents him or her and the features of that character can be acted out. As written about earlier, this metaphor of a pretend character and the child is powerful because the child can transfer the abilities and characteristics of the character to himself or herself that translate into a real-world application. For example, a child who is playing a part of a brave knight in the sand play using a knight character can explore the characteristic of being brave, and then discover ways in which he or she can be brave in real life. The therapist can emphasize these metaphors and find real-world applications for each group member. For instance, noticing that Jessica is using a knight and being brave by standing up to the leader of the band of robbers who is going to attack the castle, the therapist may tell her in the discussion phase of group, "Jessica, I noticed that you were not afraid to stand up to the bad guys in our pretend scenario today. I think since you were able to do it here today, it would be the same thing to stand up to the people that bother you at school. What do you think?"

A second benefit of using group sand and LEGO® play is that both allow for a pretend world to be created in which the child individually navigates that world but does so in the group dynamic. This gives the child the sense that he or she is not alone in their struggle, and exposes him or her to the idea that others have to face challenges and that it is okay to ask for help. As I instruct children to work together on a building task in sand or LEGO® play, I enjoy seeing how working together offers the opportunity for a child to help another child; this touches on the child's awareness not only that help is required, but also that he or she has the ability to give help. Helping another, as well as asking for help, fosters self-worth and requires self-awareness ("I can't figure this out and I need someone to show me what to do next") and it is important that the therapist design tasks within sand and LEGO® play that create opportunities for this dynamic to occur.

HOW TO STAND UP FOR MYSELF! A GROUP APPROACH TO ADDRESS BULLYING FOR YOUNGER CHILDREN

This topic shares components regarding self-worth and self-awareness, but I decided to place it in a standalone section because of its unique application to children and adolescents diagnosed with ASD. A hot topic that has received national attention in recent years is that of Bullying Prevention. It seems that every school has instituted a task force to investigate bullying complaints and to make attempts to stop bullying. While I think this is an important step, bullying has not stopped and probably will never be eradicated. Attitudes among adults such as "I was bullied and I turned out fine," and "All kids get bullied, it's just the way it is" continue to prevail and our children get caught in the seesaw between lipservice about bullying being prevented and the reality that little is actually done to prevent it. For young people diagnosed with ASD, bullying is especially prevalent. I meet with children and adolescents diagnosed with ASD regularly and it seems a new bullying story reaches my ears every day. Children and adolescents diagnosed with ASD are easy targets for bullies as these individuals tend to be isolated, can appear odd and different, and usually, these young people choose to not fight back or stand up for themselves. Young people diagnosed with ASD do not see themselves as victims in bullying scenarios and often turn their feelings inward, which leaves the young person feeling confused and more alone than ever. I am a firm believer that therapists who work with these amazing young people must equip them with emotional, mental, and physical tools to deal with the problem of bullying. While I have written about several helpful techniques to deal with bullying from an individual perspective (Hull, 2011) I will discuss some helpful ways to aid young people from a group perspective.

An Explanation of What Bullying Is

I encounter many young people, especially younger children diagnosed with ASD that have trouble distinguishing bullying behavior from non-bullying behavior. It is important to remember that children, especially those on the autism spectrum, often have difficulty distinguishing bullying behavior from non-bullying behavior. For these children, the complications that arise from mindblindness and alexithymia leave them ill-equipped to interpret the behaviors and intentions of others. I believe that it is important, especially when working with young children, to discuss what bullying is and the different forms that bullying can take. The goal is not to create a victim mind-set but to help children on the autism spectrum learn to navigate a social world that is often confusing to them. By educating children about bullying, a sense of empowerment can be instilled as well as building a foundation for coping skills.

The way I approach discussing bullying in group therapy is to talk plainly about what bullying looks like. Because bullying affects a person on physical, social, emotional, and mental levels, I discuss it from these perspectives. I tell the group members that bullying can be physical behavior or action, such as pushing, shoving, hitting, spitting, etc. It can also be social in nature, through the shunning of another person or getting others to ostracize a particular person. Bullying can also take on an emotional and mental form, through words and threatening actions that create a sense of fear and terrifying thoughts. Many bullies threaten in this manner ("I might hurt you;" "If you don't do what I want, then I'll...") which can leave a person, especially a child, in a state of continuous fear and worry.

Sharing Bullying Experiences

The group therapy setting is a great place for free discussion of members' experiences with bullies. I have found that this creates a sense of empowerment and safety in that the group members are offered the opportunity to identify with the universal struggle against bullies that seems to be so common amongst those diagnosed with ASD. I believe that when it comes to discussing bullying, allowing group members to vent and share experiences is an important element of the process of healing and learning new skills. For most young children, especially those just beginning their educational careers, bullying is a new experience. I have witnessed many children telling their story wide-eyed and shocked that other children would be so mean. Bullying is a traumatic experience and for young children to have a place to tell their story and receive affirmation of their worth and value, the long-term effects of the bullying will be minimized.

Bullying Prevention in Group Therapy with Young Children: Physical Tools

Getting to Safety!

The first physical tool that I like to introduce to children diagnosed with ASD is that of "Getting to Safety!" Many children diagnosed with ASD often "freeze" in situations in which their sense of safety is threatened and many simply turn inward, not speaking any words and not doing anything. To a bully, this behavior indicates weakness and often the bully will continue the behavior due to the appearance that the victim is not likely going to fight back or respond. Children diagnosed with ASD need to learn to overcome the paralysis and to be able to act. To work on this, I use some simple games and techniques that put children in a place of being "frozen" and then needing to quickly react. One simple game is "Duck, Duck, Goose," the age-old game of sitting in a circle while someone goes around and touches the head of the group members, who must sit completely still until "Goose!" is called and the "Goose" must jump up and try to tag the one who called them a goose. Another game that is useful is "Freeze Tag" in which members go from running to instantly being "frozen" and then back to running again. Another helpful technique is to act out a bullying situation and allow group members to walk through the scenario with the emphasis on getting away from the bully and getting to safety.

Sometimes children need to use physical force to get to safety as many young people tell me how they are cornered in a bathroom or end of a hallway or the corner of a classroom by the bully and they are confused as to what to do. Many young people diagnosed with ASD are clumsy and struggle with the coordination of movements of their bodies, and telling them to "get to safety" or "push the bully away and run" is a foreign concept. I have devised a fun exercise to help teach this concept and I call it "Give your Therapist a Good Shove!" (Hull, 2011). The group members line up and I stand at one end of the room and place an item behind me. I usually use a ball or LEGO® mini-figure, and the goal of the game is that the young person must push me out of the way and get past me and get the item. I do this in three levels: Level One, where I resist very little; Level Two where I add a bit more resistance; and, Level Three in which I provide a great deal of resistance. The purpose of this exercise has three elements: The first is to have the child practice pushing someone aside to get to safety. This puts them in the position of having done the behavior and adds a sense of familiarity with the behavior. The second element is to give the child awareness of his or her body and the force that he or she can generate. Many young people diagnosed with ASD are unaware of the force they can create with their body and many are pleasantly surprised to see their own strength. At the time of this writing I weigh two hundred and ten pounds and I assure children that if they can move me out of the way, there is little chance that they will encounter someone as big as me in their school. The third element of this exercise is that it provides a sense of self-confidence in the child's ability to defend themselves and get to safety. Many children diagnosed with ASD carry around a sense that imminent danger is right around the next corner and there is nothing that they can do about it; this exercise, however, helps to give a sense of comfort that *if* one had to get away, he or she could do so.

Tell an Adult!

Many young people diagnosed with ASD struggle with putting thoughts and feelings into words. As a result, those who are bullied often stay silent, which usually helps to perpetuate the bully's perception that the child is weak and makes the child an easy target. One easy exercise to practice in group therapy is pretending to tell an adult. The therapist should walk the group members through the process of getting the adult's attention and then have a short explanation of what happened, who was hurting or threatening them, and what was said or done. While this may seem very simple to a neurotypical individual, it can be very hard for a young person diagnosed with ASD. The adult may be a teacher, school official, church official, or parent. Regardless of whom the person is, helping our young people feel confident and comfortable to speak up about what is happening to them is an important part of helping them become self-confident.

Bullying Prevention in Group Therapy with Young Children: Mental Tools

Think Powerful! I Don't Have to Let Someone Hurt Me!

It is important to give young people cognitive tools when it comes to bullying prevention. How one thinks has a large impact on his or her feelings and subsequent behavior. I have found that equipping young people with a positive, strong mind-set gives them a solid foundation from which positive emotions and behaviors can spring, and then bullying behavior has less of an impact on the young person. One way that I have helped get this across is through the use of Superheroes, as many children like Superheroes and are at least familiar with them. Rubin (2007) has made an excellent contribution to the world of play therapy literature that uses Superheroes, and some of this idea sprang from reading his work. I say to the group members while holding a Superman or Batman character, "Imagine if Batman thought he was a loser and that he would be beaten by a pipsqueak!" Usually the group members laugh at the thought of Batman thinking such a ridiculous thought, but it gets the point across that when a person thinks he or she is weak or will be beaten, they usually do not do very well. I reinforce the thought "I don't have to let someone hurt me" and that rationale behind the thought. This helps to build up the child's sense of self-worth and strengthens the foundational belief system that it is not okay to be abused.

Think Smart! "I Can Get Help—I'm Not Alone!"

Another thought I like to incorporate into bullying prevention when addressing the cognitive tools is that of "I can get help—I'm not alone!" This thought is important in helping to reinforce the truth that the young person is not alone in the world, that there is always someone to reach out to for help. Due to the tendency that I mentioned earlier in which young people diagnosed with ASD struggle with putting thoughts and feelings into words, many stay silent, reinforcing a core belief that they are alone in their struggle with the bully or bullies and there is nothing that can be done. By reinforcing the thought "I am not alone" a positive, truth-based belief is formed that results in the young person being more likely to reach out and communicate what is going on. This concept can be communicated through any number of metaphors such as Superheroes (The Avengers, Batman and Robin), Barbie Dolls (Barbie and her Friends), or LEGO® mini-figures.

Bullying Prevention in Group Therapy with Young Children: Emotional Tools

Overcoming Fear!

Children diagnosed with ASD who are being bullied need tools to deal with the emotions that arise as a result of being threatened or hurt. Perhaps the most common emotional reaction is fear, and the cascade effects of fear range from being paralyzed and staying silent, to believing that there is nothing one can do. Perhaps one of the greatest tools that a child can learn in overcoming fear is the ability to self-soothe and to learn to relax. Perhaps the simplest way to teach relaxation is through teaching the child to breathe effectively. Cabe (2001) has described an excellent technique to help young people learn effective breathing through the use of blowing bubbles. The technique begins with the therapist filling the room with bubbles, which children will usually try to pop. The therapist then instructs the group members to blow one large bubble to get the feeling of deep, slow breaths. The group members are encouraged to continue working on blowing as big a bubble as possible. The therapist will then provide an explanation of how when fear sets in, the brain triggers the body to tell it that it needs more air, but the lungs are already overwhelmed from the fear. The good news is that by breathing slowly and deeply the brain will be able send the message to the lungs to naturally slow down, and as the lungs work better, the body will naturally relax (Cabe, 2001). I have used this technique and found that it is very effective in teaching children about how the body works in a fun way.

A second technique in helping children diagnosed with ASD to overcome their fear related to bullies is to help them formulate an "Escape Plan." The Escape Plan is a series of steps that the child will take *if* a bully is encountered. Much like an evacuation plan in a house or place of business in case of fire or other disaster, the Escape Plan involves taking the exact steps that the child would take to get out of danger and to safety. The goal is that the fear caused by *what if* will be replaced with confidence as a result of the child knowing what he or she could do in case a bully is encountered. I have used this technique with great success in individual therapy as well as group, and I have the group members draw out the situation and then write the steps underneath the scenario or on the side of the paper. Each group member is asked to show their Escape Plan and be able to remember all the steps.

Using Anger as Positive Energy!

One problematic emotion that results from bullying is anger, and children diagnosed with ASD need tools to process anger and direct the anger towards the situation, not at themselves. Young people diagnosed with ASD tend to internalize feelings, especially anger. I have encountered many who become very angry about the bullying behavior *after* the encounter, but this negative emotion does nothing more than create frustration and self-loathing. The goal in group therapy is to help the members understand that by directing their anger at the situation instead of themselves, the anger can become positive energy that can be used to do something productive. The therapist explains that some of the productive ways the energy can be used is to communicate about the incident to a peer, or an adult such as a parent. The young person can also channel the energy towards something that he or she enjoys, such as art, video/computer games, or music. The bubble-breath technique that was previously discussed in dealing with fear is also very helpful to teach children a way to deal with anger.

Chapter Five

Group Therapy with Older Children Diagnosed with ASD

I have chosen to devote a separate chapter to group therapy with older children diagnosed with ASD as I believe that the emotional and psychological needs of older children are unique enough that specific techniques are warranted. The same sections of emotional issues, perspective-taking, self-worth/self-awareness, and bullying prevention will be covered, but additional techniques will be discussed that are tailored for the more advanced developmental abilities of older children. Remember that when it comes to children diagnosed with ASD, the concept of age as it relates to the number of years a person has been on the planet becomes irrelevant; the therapist must assess the child's emotional and mental capacity and abilities and take into account which group therapy setting will be most beneficial.

GROUP THERAPY APPLIED TO EMOTIONAL ISSUES OF OLDER CHILDREN ON THE AUTISM SPECTRUM

Older children diagnosed with ASD often struggle with emotions such as fear, frustration, and sadness. Because of the challenges related to alexithymia, negative emotions are often confusing and can leave the young person in a crippled state. Further complicating things is that adults have higher expectations for older children when it comes to emotional control. There is a cultural expectation that a child of twelve *should* be able to exhibit better emotional control than a five-year-old; yet for those diagnosed with ASD what is expected and what the young person is capable of do not always match. While older children diagnosed with ASD typically do have more emotional coping skills than younger children, we must remember how quickly these young people are triggered by negative emotions and that once the "fight-or-flight" system is triggered it is very difficult for the young person to calm down again. I often remind parents and teachers the importance of staying calm and non-reactive to the child's emotional volatility as humans are biologically wired to match the anxiety level of those around them (Badenoch & Bogdan, 2012). The group therapy experience is a wonderful way to help older children gain a better understanding of emotions and learn skills to tolerate negative emotions.

The Use of UNO to Understand Emotions

I discussed how to use colors to help explain emotions to young children diagnosed with ASD. This technique is similar but incorporates the use of the game UNO. UNO is an easy, fairly quick game that is wonderfully suited for the group setting. UNO uses the basic colors of red, blue, green, and yellow. I assign the following emotions to its corresponding color: Red = Anger; Yellow = Calm/Happy; Blue = Sad; Green = Frustrated. The cards are dealt to each player and the game begins. When a card is laid down, the player who laid the card down must identify the emotion represented by its corresponding color and share something personal related to that emotion. For example, Peter lays down a green card. He says, "Green means frustrated. I get frustrated when my little sister interrupts me and then my parents yell at me for telling her to shut up and wait." The point of this is to simply get the group members to recognize emotions and to identify an experience when they felt that emotion. Through this process, the members connect the experience and the emotion which lays a foundation for the therapist to begin to teach coping skills to deal with problematic emotions. For example, a follow-up question for Peter would be, "So tell me what happens after you tell your little sister to shut up?" Peter then explains that he loses his video game privilege and when the therapist asks how he feels when his privilege is taken, Peter promptly answers, "Angry!" The therapist can use this information to discuss choices and how Peter went from frustrated to angry (as demonstrated by a red UNO card) based on his choices. This part of the technique helps group members see the connections between choices and consequences and the various emotions that arise from both.

A surrising discovery occurred when I began using this technique with young people diagnosed with ASD. It offered the opportunity to discuss sadness. I have found that for children diagnosed with ASD, the emotion of sadness is rarely discussed, at least much less so than anger or frustration. One of the main reasons is that parents, teachers, and therapists tend to focus on the emotions that lead to poor choices and negative consequences such as anger; thus, sadness is often left out of the equation. However, in this technique, each time a Blue card is laid down group members are given the opportunity to talk about being sad and the various events and circumstances which trigger sad feelings. Children diagnosed with ASD often feel sad but have a hard time putting those feelings into words, and many do not appear sad or "down" because of their difficulty in showing emotions through facial gestures and body language. Thus, parents, teachers, and other caregivers often miss the buildup of this key emotion, which has a tendency to accumulate and create feelings of despair and self-loathing. I also like this use of the game UNO because there is an emphasis on joy/happiness which is also helpful to identify, instead of just negative emotions.

The technique can be modified so that after group members are comfortable with identifying emotions and sharing experiences about those emotions, the therapist can then move on to coping skills. For example, if Susan lays down a Blue card (sadness) she must say one positive behavior that she can do when she is sad or a coping skill to deal with sadness. As the game of UNO is played, each group member is given the opportunity to come up with coping skills for negative emotions and also have the benefit to listen to how others cope with sadness, anger, and frustration. This dynamic also helps with perspective-taking and reinforces the idea that "I am not alone" in dealing with negative feelings. I have had many parents and caregivers remark to me that they noticed an improvement in their young person diagnosed with ASD in regards to coping with negative emotions and also being able to talk about the "triggers" that spawn negative reactions.

The Worry Can

Hall, Kaduson, and Schaefer (2002) describe the use of a "worry can" as a way to deal with children's fears and worry. The technique can also be used with other negative emotions such as sadness, frustration, and anger. The therapist uses a can or bucket (any receptacle will do) and places a label on the side. Children can be allowed to create the label or draw pictures on the label that represent worry or fear. The group members all discuss what worries them and are given pieces of paper on which they can write out their fear or worry. The fear or worry may be drawn if the child does not want to write. Children diagnosed with ASD sometimes struggle with writing and do much better expressing themselves with symbols or pictures. The fears or worries of each child are discussed and then the pieces of paper are put into the can. Hall, Kaduson, and Schaefer (2002) suggest putting a lid on the can and using strips of paper which are slid through a slot in the top of the can; however, I simply leave the can open on top and have the children ball up the paper and toss it into the can. I have found that wadding up a piece of paper can be very empowering for children and adolescents.

The power of this exercise is that it creates a visual picture of an internalized worry or fear becoming external (through writing it down, drawing it, and discussing it) and then being balled up and tossed away, as if the fear or worry is physically removed from the child's life. The therapist can also create a "Solution Can" in which positive and creative solutions are placed and then drawn out and read or acted out as a way for the group members to learn coping skills to combat fear and worry. This technique allows children to express their fear or worry and also creates the opportunity for children to solve their own problems and help others as well. I am constantly amazed by children diagnosed with ASD in their ability to strategize solutions to problems both for themselves and others in the group format, and this technique is one that helps create a stage for such a wonderful phenomenon.

Balloon Breathing, Nice and Slow!

It is important to teach young people the important role that breathing plays in preventing stress and dealing with overwhelming emotions. I am passionate about giving young people, especially those diagnosed with ASD tools that help them self-soothe. This technique involves having the group members blow up a balloon much like the technique that was described in the section for young children. While that technique was more designed to deal with anger, this technique prepares group members to use the blowing up of the balloon as a model for deep, even breathing that can be practiced anytime the young person is feeling stress or overwhelmed. Due to the fact that individuals diagnosed with ASD are "triggered" constantly, learning to breathe effectively is of vital importance in facing fears and taking risks, like trying something new or entering a new social situation. Each member is given a balloon and is told to blow the balloon up slowly. I usually demonstrate the technique for them, and show them how the lungs, when filled, expand through the whole midsection and can take in a great deal of air. As I blow up the balloon, I demonstrate how slowly releasing the air creates a sort of "woozy" feeling in my head, but that is simply the rush of oxygen-rich blood reaching the brain. I use the technique to teach how slow, rhythmic breathing helps the lungs and heart reduce their "frantic" pace, which results in a calming effect in the brain and body. Once this has been done several times, the therapist can reinforce how good breathing is a defense against feeling stressed and emotionally overwhelmed.

GAMES THAT HELP IN LEARNING TO DEAL WITH FRUSTRATION

I mentioned the use of board games in group therapy in chapter 4. While virtually any board game can be used as a tool to help learn to tolerate frustration, one game that I really like and use often with older children is Bop It! Smash (Special Edition) by Hasbro Games. Bop It! can be used in a single player mode or multi-player mode. The game involves attempting to stop a series of blinking lights at the right time by hitting the end of the tube on either end with either the left or right hand or both. The player holds the device in both hands and activates the game by hitting either end of the device. The device uses a series of sounds and when the player gets the light to stop in the middle, a voice calls out encouragement such as "Yes!" and when the player misses, the voice will say something like, "Oh man, try again!" If the player misses numerous times, the voice becomes more negative. I use the game in individual therapy as a way to help young people learn to fight off negative messages sent by others by engaging in positive self-talk. The game is useful in the group setting by helping group members learn to offer praise and encouragement, as well as learning to ignore negative messages and overcome frustration. Multi-player mode is useful in group therapy as each player is able to take a turn, and if done successfully, passes the device to the next person. If a player is not successful on their first try, he or she is given three chances to stop the blinking light at the correct point. After three unsuccessful tries, the player is "out," and gradually there is only one player standing.

While I congratulate the "winner" I refrain from making any game in group therapy about winning or losing. The focus is always on the tool that is gained from the experience and I emphasize the metaphor from the activity that translates into the group members' real lives. Bop It! Smash helps group members practice the skill of focusing on an activity while blocking out negative comments and dealing with frustration. The emotion of frustration is the main catalyst in creating a snowball of negative thoughts and behaviors for individuals diagnosed with ASD. The fear of not knowing how to handle frustration keeps many of these remarkable people captive and afraid to venture out of safe routines and to have the confidence to try new things. Early interventions in helping young people diagnosed with ASD learn strategies to deal with frustration will help them on their developmental journey towards maturity.

Video/Computer Games

I wrote in chapter 4 how useful video/computer games can be to help young children diagnosed with ASD learn to deal with negative emotions, increase perspective-taking skills, and instill a greater sense of self-worth and self-confidence. Video/computer games are a great tool in group therapy with older children in each of the above areas as well, but particularly in the area of learning to deal with negative emotions such as anger, frustration, and fear. Older children of both sexes are familiar with all kinds of video/computer games and in many ways the games represent a common language that connects young people from all walks of life. Gaming consoles such as the

Wii and XBOX Kinect offer a group therapist many tools that can be used in the group format (some of which will be discussed in later chapters). In this section, I will discuss one game that I have used much in group therapy to help older children diagnosed with ASD deal with negative emotions: MineCraft.

MineCraft: A Group Approach

Any therapist who has been working with young people in the last few years has witnessed the explosion of the popularity of the game MineCraft. Young people of all ages and even adults have been drawn to the game's unique appearance and story. The game can be played in a tablet and smartphone format, gaming console such as the XBOX 360, and there is a PC version as well. I use the PC version in my group therapy sessions and set up a laptop on a table with chairs around the table for the group members. This allows for one player to play while the other group members watch, and then the players can rotate so that each gets to sit in the "commander's" chair and be in charge of the controls.

The basic design of MineCraft is that the player is allowed to enter a "world" complete with terrain such as mountains, deserts, and lush forests surrounded by lakes, rivers, and oceans. The player is able to use basic geological elements and "mine" the elements using common tools and create materials that the player can use to create buildings and other necessities that are necessary for survival. There are two modes that a player may choose from: Creative mode or Survival mode. Creative mode allows the player to wander through the MineCraft "universe" and create and explore as he or she wishes without threats from enemies or any loss of energy. Survival mode is the more realistic playing experience in which the player must defend against enemies (zombies, creepers, ender-men, and giant spiders) and stay nourished so that the player's "health" is intact. The player can "die" in Survival mode, usually due to a surprise attack from zombies or other enemies, and there is an array of weapons (swords, bow and arrows, etc.) that the player can use to fight off enemies. I find that young people diagnosed with ASD are attracted to MineCraft due to the ability to be completely in charge of the "universe" and be able to create their own personal world.

As previously mentioned, I use MineCraft in group therapy to help young people learn to overcome negative emotions. To do this, I focus on the enemies of the game: zombies, creepers, ender-men, and giant spiders. I allow each group member to name the negative emotion that is most problematic for them using an enemy name from the game. For instance, Johnny might refer to his anger as a zombie, which helps to give a visual picture to the emotion. The "enemies" are metaphors for negative emotions such as anger, frustration, and fear. I then have the group members notice the "tools" that are used to defeat the enemies such as swords, bows and arrows, and fire. However, I also point out that a player can also avoid the enemies by being aware and avoiding them by running away. I explain how negative emotions are connected to irrational, negative thoughts and give the group members some examples. I then explain that the "tools" in defeating negative emotions are to think positive, truth-based thoughts, and I have each group member identify a negative, irrational thought that is connected to a negative emotion. I then have them plug in a positive, truth-based thought and have them identify the positive emotion that surfaces. Thinking about the connection between thoughts and feelings can be a hard concept for any child, whether he or she is diagnosed with ASD or neurotypical. However, using the metaphors from the game which the children love provides a picture that helps them to understand the concept.

Timmy and Frustration: "A Creeper that I Can Beat!"

Timmy was part of a group of eleven- and twelve-year-olds and like many young people diagnosed with ASD, he struggled with the emotion of frustration. Timmy quickly became emotional at the slightest irritation, like when the green beans on his plate accidentally touched the mashed potatoes, or if his socks "bunched" around his toes in his sneakers. These irritations usually resulted in him verbally or physically lashing out, which of course led to consequences. Timmy loved MineCraft and was ecstatic that it was going to be used as part of group therapy; and I vividly remember the day Timmy's group was introduced to the metaphor of negative emotions being seen as enemies because it represented a turning point for Timmy. Timmy visualized frustration as a "creeper" and described the state of him being frustrated as "creeper mode." Immediately upon being given this visualization of frustration with a familiar image from his beloved game, it was as if Timmy was handed a powerful tool that gave him the strength and awareness to begin to learn to control his frustration. His mother remarked to me that he would tell her he was working hard to stay out of "creeper mode" when he was beginning to get frustrated and that he could verbalize the feeling of the oncoming frustration, which was a new skill for him. This foundation paved the way for Timmy to learn coping skills or "tools" to control his frustration and avoid being in the "dungeon;" his term for getting in trouble. One day when sharing about his most recent triumph over frustration with his group members, he said, "Frustration is a creeper that I can beat!"

GROUP THERAPY APPLIED TO INCREASING PERSPECTIVE-TAKING IN OLDER CHILDREN ON THE AUTISM SPECTRUM

I have written much about the problems that individuals diagnosed with ASD have with perspective-taking, also known as mindblindness or Theory of Mind (ToM) deficits. Older children diagnosed with ASD approaching adolescence encounter more complicated social situations and higher social expectations of parents, teachers, and other adults. Mindblindness disrupts the ability of the young person diagnosed with ASD to form deeper, long-lasting friendships that usually begin to form in older childhood. Thus, the young person diagnosed with ASD feels as though he or she is on the sidelines watching the flurry of relationship building going on around them, wanting to join in but not knowing how to do so. The techniques that follow are designed to help older children diagnosed with ASD increase perspective-taking so that they can better navigate the increasingly complicated social world that surrounds them.

Thought Bubble Training

I wrote in chapter 4 about the usefulness of thought-bubble training with younger children diagnosed with ASD in group therapy. Older children can also benefit from thought-bubble training in group therapy. This technique is conducted in a similar manner as described in chapter 4 with younger children, but I alter the technique based on the interests and abilities of the group members. For example, one group happened to love comic books and reading Manga so I gave each member a piece of paper with lines dividing the page into separate cells, much like a comic storyboard. Each group member was asked to describe a situation involving another person or persons that was problematic or anxiety provoking and then I instructed the members to draw the characters using stick figures in the cells complete with the thinking bubbles that are left blank. Each member was asked to fill in the thought bubble and imagine what the other person was thinking and what he or she was thinking during the encounter. The group then discussed each member's story and I helped those who had difficulty imagining what the other people might be thinking. During this phase I use a white board on which I can easily erase facial expressions and show how facial expressions can reveal what a person may be thinking.

While the group described above liked the storyboard approach due to their love of comics and Manga, others may not understand this format and will do better with the technique as described in chapter 4. The therapist should be prepared to offer prompts to help the group members get started and many require individual help from the therapist. If I encounter a great deal of resistance or confusion, I use my white board and remind myself to go slowly. For neurotypical individuals, perspective-taking is a naturally occurring ability and it is easy to become impatient with those who struggle with this concept. The therapist must remember that the goal is not to magically "cure" mindblindness, but to simply get the young person familiar with the idea of imagining what another person might be thinking. Patience on the part of the therapist is of utmost importance when using a technique such as this.

The Shoe Switch Game: Putting on Another's Shoes

I am constantly thinking about techniques and applications of those techniques to help the young people diagnosed with ASD with whom I work. One day, while listening to a friend talk about a misunderstanding with a family member, he made the comment that the family member seemed unable to "put himself in someone else's shoes." I got the idea from this conversation to actually have my group members change shoes with each other in order to imagine what it may be like to see things from another's perspective. However, some of the group members were appalled at the idea of putting their feet in someone else's shoes so I came up with the idea of having each group member stand on a large piece of paper and tracing their shoes with a marker and then writing the member's name on the paper. I found that an added bonus to this was that I could write the group member's thoughts and feelings on the paper as well, based on the situation that was being discussed. For example, Scott shared a story about being bullied at school. As he shared, I wrote down some of the thoughts and feelings on the paper above where his feet were traced. Stephanie, another group member, volunteered to stand in Scott's shoes to imagine what it would be like to experience the event from Scott's perspective. Standing on the paper, Stephanie is able to look down and read some of Scott's thoughts and feelings that help to shift her perspective. The final part of the technique is asking each member what it was like to be "in someone else's shoes" as well as to ask them to come up with coping skills to get through the situation. The above scenario actually occurred during a group session that I conducted and was very successful in helping the member who was being bullied gather coping skills to deal with the bullies. Conversely, the other group members remarked that they were surprised at the boy's strength in being able to get through such a hard situation. The exercise spawned conversation regarding empathy and provided an excellent visual representation of perspective-taking. One group member remarked, "I knew that things were hard for me but I had no idea that other people had such a hard time too."

IMPROVING PERSPECTIVE-TAKING THROUGH VIDEO/ COMPUTER GAME GROUP PLAY

"Why didn't you go down that pipe?" Conner asks, annoyed. "Because I'm going to get the Warp Whistle so we can warp to World Four," Jonathan replies, casually scratching his head while still holding the controller and moving Mario up and over a wall. "Oh," Conner says, his eyes riveted on Jonathan's progress. The boys are playing a version of Super Mario Bros. "I didn't know there was a Warp Whistle in this level," Conner said, briefly looking over at Jonathan. "Yes, there is," replied Jonathan. "And if you go down the pipe you're too far back and you'll miss the chance to get the Whistle. The first time I tried this I was scared that it wouldn't work and then I'd be mad that I wasted a life." "I was scared too," Jalen piped in, "because I didn't think you could really do it. But then I tried it and now I do it every time. Hey, Jonathan, nice job on finishing the level," said Jalen, clapping his hands. "Thanks," Jonathan replied. "I'm glad to know you guys are scared to try new things in games too," said Conner, shivering slightly. I don't like trying new things unless I'm really sure or someone shows me." "I think that's how everyone feels," Jonathan said, handing the controller to Conner. "Really? That's a relief," Conner sighed, taking the controller and pushing a button to begin a new level.

The above exchange demonstrates how video games played in a group therapy format can help introduce the concept of perspective-taking in young people diagnosed with ASD. The exchange I have written is based on a real conversation that took place during group video game play without any direction from me. The boys were simply in play and observing the different ways that each of them interacted with the game. For example, one may not choose to get any coins or attributes, but simply be focused on "completing the level;" another player may be interested in getting every item on the way to the completion of the stage. Some play fast, some much slower, but I have noticed that each plays in his or her own style. This observation led to the idea that group video/computer game play could be used to teach perspective-taking in those diagnosed with ASD.

Group video/computer game play in the group therapy format is helpful in teaching perspective-taking. The major reason is that the members are observing the behavior and actions of others. Group members watch the action of a player and are directed by the therapist to notice the differences of that player compared to how he or she would play the game. Because the game is something that the young person finds interesting, he or she has a context of meaning for the idea of shifting perspective. For example, Sarah watches Ben play a level of a game that she enjoys but finds difficult. Ben, who is prompted by the therapist to teach Sarah the steps to completing the level, shows Sarah techniques and strategies. This activity forces Sarah to watch Ben's behavior and listen to what he saying, and then gives her the opportunity to put into practice what has been seen and heard. Depending on the game that is being used, connections can be made between the themes in the games and real-life scenarios that the group members are dealing with.

Another important part of this technique is that the therapist can stop the action at any time, which helps to focus the group members' attention to the task and redirect if need be or answer questions that have arisen. It is important for the therapist to stop the action frequently to reinforce a certain concept, or to redirect the focus of the group members when their attention span wanes. One of the joys I experience in using young people's specified interests in the therapy process is the interests create a natural process of motivation towards skill acquisition. While the play and skill acquisition of young people diagnosed with ASD is different from neurotypical peers (Rubin, 2012), it is important that therapists who work with these amazing individuals combine the use of imagination and the specified interests of the young people in seeking to pull them up the developmental ladder by introducing new skills.

GROUP THERAPY APPLIED TO INCREASING SELF-WORTH AND SELF-AWARENESS FOR OLDER CHILDREN ON THE AUTISM SPECTRUM

As children mature, they are exposed to great social pressures and more complicated patterns of social interaction. As children near adolescence, the physical, emotional, and mental changes that happen in their bodies create stress and emotional insecurity typically begins to arise. For older children diagnosed with ASD, encountering the greater social pressures and complicated patterns of social interaction can come as a surprise and many appear to be "left behind" socially and developmentally. It is important for therapists working with young people diagnosed with ASD to recognize that the young person is not deficient, but simply delayed. The typical milestones that neurotypical young people reach at older childhood are often out of reach for the young person diagnosed with ASD; however, it must be remembered that skills can be taught and with sufficient time, the young person can reach these necessary developmental milestones. However, what is often most at risk for both neurotypical young people and those diagnosed with ASD is that their sense of self-worth can become shattered during this time of life. The therapist must work to encourage family members and caregivers to protect and nurture the child's sense of self-worth. The techniques that follow will help with increasing the self-worth and self-awareness of older children diagnosed with ASD.

Show and Tell

While most people think of "Show and Tell" as an activity for younger children, I find that young people of all ages enjoy showing peers something that is dear to them. One does not need to look very far on popular social networking sites such as Facebook or Pinterest to see that adults are no different in their desire to share what is meaningful in their daily life. I discussed the value of "Show and Tell" in group therapy with younger children, and the activity is used in a similar way for older children. However, one element that I include when using "Show and Tell" with older children is a social skill component. Since older children are expected to be more verbal and more adept at navigating social situations, I use the "Show and Tell" activity to prompt the older child diagnosed with ASD to speak clearly and plainly, make eye contact, and also to answer questions regarding their item of interest. Repetition and practice are essential in gaining social skills and the group therapy environment is an excellent place to do so. Because group members are showing something that they are knowledgeable about and naturally like, there is a good deal of internal motivation to follow the prompts of the therapist in practicing public speaking. During this activity, I make sure group members know that most people do not like speaking in front of a group and that even entertainers struggle with fear right before taking the stage.

Pass the Ball

This technique is also helpful with older children as well as younger children in helping to encourage group participation and to get group members comfortable about speaking in a group setting. The technique also gives the group members a chance to "have the floor" and share thoughts and feelings without being interrupted which helps to increase the child's sense of self-worth. "Pass the Ball" is also a good grounding exercise at the beginning of group to help with the transition of entering the group therapy room and settling the group into the routine. Two of the groups that I conduct are in the afternoon after school, and many of the young people are tired and restless. Sitting on the floor in a circle and using the ball to regulate whose turn it is to speak helps the group members relax and get into the flow of the group therapy process.

The Slow Motion Game

Many children diagnosed with ASD have difficulty with impulsivity. Many children on the autism spectrum possess great mental and emotional energy that translates into attention deficits for things that the young person finds unappealing and also generates attentive intensiveness towards specified interests. Many children diagnosed with ASD also struggle with transitioning from one activity to another—for example, stopping one activity and starting another. These transition stages are the times when many make poor choices due to impulsivity. Hall, and others (2002) created the "Slow Motion Game" in order to help children with impulse control problems learn to "slow" down and gain impulse control skills through practice and repetition. I have used this with great success in individual therapy to teach impulse control skills for neurotypical children and those diagnosed with ASD, and have found it to be very useful in the group therapy format as well. For children diagnosed with ASD and who struggle with perspective-taking, the technique can be valuable in increasing the child's sense of self-awareness and self-control.

The technique is simple and easy to use, and most young people find the exercise fun. The therapist creates scenarios that are written down on cards that are placed face down. These are simple everyday tasks such as walking to the refrigerator, doing jumping jacks, or doing a math problem. The therapist sets a timer for one minute and calls out when ten seconds are left. The goal is for the group member to act out the activity as slowly as possible. After the group members get the idea of the technique, I use scenarios that I know represent challenges in the lives of the group members, such as "Your sister throws a sock and hits you in the face. Show us in slow motion what you should say and do that is a good choice." The group members take turns and can earn tokens or chips for completing the activity with the opportunity to earn a treat or small prize at the end of the exercise.

I add an extra cognitive/behavioral dimension to the technique by "freezing" the action in the middle of a group member's turn and asking what he or she is thinking at that moment. This attaches a thinking component to the exercise in addition to the behavioral action of slowly acting through a situation. I have also used this in family counseling with families who have members diagnosed with ASD to work through a problem situation slowly in order to process thoughts and feelings and to help introduce emotional coping skills and model impulse control. The overall goal is that group members experience three things. First, that he or she can learn to control behavioral impulses. Many young people diagnosed with ASD often view behaviors, as well as the thoughts and feelings that go along with them, as foreign objects that are "out of my control." Second, it is important that the young person experience the process of slowing down long enough to think through a behavior. By making slow, purposeful movements, group members can grasp the benefit of going slowly. Third, the technique allows the group member to replay a situation that has caused problems in the past in order to become more self-aware. This can lead to a greater sense of self-worth and self-confidence in facing the situation again.

HOW TO STAND UP FOR MYSELF! A GROUP APPROACH TO ADDRESS BULLYING FOR OLDER CHILDREN

Bullying tends to take on new forms as children move towards late childhood and adolescence. For boys, there is more physical threatening, and for girls, the emotional and mental jabs of other girls become more complex and intense. The characteristics of ASD such as deficits in joint attention, mind-blindness, and alexithymia create great challenges in the young person forming and sustaining relationships. Peers of older children, who are themselves immature and unable to frame into any meaningful context the often odd-appearing behaviors of those diagnosed with ASD, seek to reject that which is not understood and usually this rejection is done through bullying. Bullying affects a person on physical, emotional, mental, and spiritual levels, for it brings a sense of despair and, ultimately, self-rejection through self-loathing. Older children diagnosed with ASD, who are already confused by the quickly shifting social landscape and feel as though they are watching from the sidelines, tend to sum up social deficiencies as "my fault" and turn their negative emotions such as anger and sadness inward. These emotions fester, creating inner mental and emotional turmoil and deeper self-loathing. Because of the difficulty in putting thoughts and feelings into words, the young person sinks to a place of deep despair and hopelessness. While all children are subjected to bullying in some form, those diagnosed with ASD are affected more severely because many often feel as though they have no one to help them in their journey.

The group therapy experience can be not only a safe place for older children who are bullied, but a rich environment in which the young person can learn and grow. Much like the experience of younger children in group therapy, older children can greatly benefit from knowing that others have a similar struggle and many find hope in the confines of group therapy. The techniques that follow are designed to guide the young person to learning to cope with bullying behavior, to better understand himself or herself, and to build up a sense of value and worth so that the words and actions of the bully carry less weight if this behavior is encountered in the future. This section will cover three main areas: Physical, mental, and emotional, and each section will provide the group therapist with techniques that will give group members valuable tools for this ever-present problem.

Bullying Prevention in Group Therapy with Older Children: Physical Tools

Older children diagnosed with ASD need physical tools to help them feel confident in facing bullying behavior and to instill a sense of safety in navigating their everyday life. The following techniques are designed help group members learn about their bodies and be able to use their bodies to ask for help, get to safety, and learn to value themselves in new ways. Ultimately, these techniques are about empowering the young people and helping them remove the fear of bullies from their life so they can be free to learn, grow, and express themselves in their unique way. No human being should have to live in fear of another, especially at a time in life when there is so much to experience.

Getting to Safety! Red Light, Green Light!

I discussed in chapter 4 how many young people diagnosed with ASD become "frozen" when confronted with a bullying situation. Many young people share with me how they felt "rooted" to the floor and that their her body would not respond when the big, mean bully was staring them down. I also wrote how many children diagnosed with ASD lack body awareness; many appear "detached" from recognizing various signals in their body, or noticing that their bodies have the capability to do certain things. I discussed in chapter 4 how "Getting to Safety" is an important part of dealing with bullying behavior. Physical movement, and more importantly, purposeful movement, has been found to be an important deterrent to predators, such as rapists or kidnappers. I tell the young people who come to me that when people look at a body, a body that is moving appears larger and more powerful than a body that is sitting still, or "frozen." Because many individuals diagnosed with ASD do not feel comfortable with eye contact, bullies often interpret this behavior as weakness. Therefore, it is important for the therapist to help the young person to realize how important body movement and eye contact are in warding off bullying threats.

"Getting to Safety! Red Light, Green Light!" is a technique that combines these elements of being determined and reacting quickly. The technique or "game" is played in the traditional manner but with some therapeutic modifications. The "leader" stands at the front of the group while the other players line up some distance away. This technique obviously requires a large room or outside space. The traditional game has the leader standing with his or her back turned to the group, but in this version, I have the leader face the group. The leader calls out either "Green Light," meaning go or run towards the leader, or "Red Light," meaning stop. The leader holds a ribbon or stick in his hand and the goal of the game is to be the first one to grab the stick from the leader's hand. The stick can also be placed at the leader's feet if he or she is uncomfortable having someone take something from their hand. I say this because sometimes there is a mad rush towards the leader and having the stick or item at his or her feet avoids the problem of potentially being mobbed. I inform the group members that they must keep eye contact with the leader at all times, and that they must listen carefully for the instructions of the leader. I also tell each member to pay close attention to their bodies and notice the sensation of bursting into action from a complete stop. The technique is a fun way to practice the action of moving quickly in a determined, purposeful way, and gives group members a sensation of what it feels like to get his or her body moving quickly. I share with the group members that when encountered with a bullying situation that is physically threatening, the most important part is getting to safety and that this requires quick, purposeful action.

Give Your Therapist a Good Shove!

This technique that was discussed in chapter 4 is also a good one to use with older children. The goal is the same: Group members learn to generate force with their body and to use that force to move past a person in order to get to a goal. The members are reminded that this is only used in emergency situations and when he or she has encountered a threat, such as a bully, and are cornered with nowhere to go. This technique is useful in helping to overcome the paralysis that often occurs in young people diagnosed with ASD when they come in contact with a bully.

Sword Fights: Be Bold and Ready for Action!

Children of all ages are familiar with swords. Star Wars used a version of the sword with the infamous light saber and the Pirates of the Caribbean movies cemented swords in the pantheon of "cool" weaponry. I use foam, play swords in my work with all children, from neurotypical children to those diagnosed with ASD and I have found them to be helpful for releasing feelings such as anger and frustration, but also to teach the kinetics of body motion. I have mentioned that children diagnosed with ASD often lack body awareness, and I have discovered that sword play is a great way to coordinate movement in the hands, arms, trunk, and legs of the child. It is relatively easy and inexpensive to make a foam sword. A helpful instruction manual is available here: http://www.wikihow.com/Make-a-Boffer-(Foam-Sword). Any time the therapist is using a simulated weapon in the therapy process, it is a good idea to have some rules. One, no hitting a person's body (the sword strike can only occur on the opponent's sword and vice-versa). Two, any purposeful blow to a person's body, particularly the head, face, or private parts results in a loss of turn and possibly being banned from the game. Sometimes children diagnosed with ASD struggle with impulse control and it is important that each group member understands that no one is going to turn into Captain Jack Sparrow. Three, the object of the swordplay is to engage in the simulation of sword fighting but the goal is not to "beat" anyone or hurt anyone. I have found it is helpful to have the members count aloud as the swords touch, counting up to the number five and then starting over. This focus on counting tends to keep their minds off "winning" and prevents aggression and can also direct their attention to their body's movement and moving with the motion of the sword.

The members are divided into groups of two and a sword is given to each. If the room is a smaller space, the therapist may want to limit the sparring to two at a time while the rest of the group watches, and then rotate the members so that each gets a turn. The therapist should encourage the group members to notice the movement of their bodies. For example, I demonstrate how a powerful stance (arms out, legs shoulder-width apart, etc.) protects my body and sends the message that "I am ready!" I also demonstrate how the body has a flow in that as I move my right leg forward the right arm naturally wants to extend. Sometimes I will show a Star Wars film clip to demonstrate the motion and flow. This technique is useful in helping young people diagnosed with ASD learn about their body's movements and become familiar with the sensation of a body in motion, which helps with body awareness. Another useful part of this technique is that it contains a combat element in that two group members are "facing off" and can help build the confidence of a young person that is being bullied physically. I have found that by allowing a young person to practice standing up to an opponent in a situation such as this, it helps him or her prepare for life in the real world.

Bullying Prevention in Group Therapy with Older Children: Mental Tools

I wrote in chapter 4 about the importance of fostering a child's mental strength in regards to bullying. I often tell young people in my office that the brain is the biggest muscle in the body, and the ability to think clearly and quickly can be stronger than a boxer's right hook. I am passionate about equipping young people with mental tools that assist them in the struggle against bullying behavior.

Devise a Safety Plan!

Every major building in the United States, from banks and schools to businesses, has a disaster emergency escape plan posted somewhere in the building. We are told that our homes should have a similar escape plan in case of fire or other disaster. It is also helpful to have children diagnosed with ASD who are experiencing bullying to have a mental "disaster escape plan" when it comes to dealing with the potential threat. In the event of disasters, having a well-thought-out plan "in case" has proven to be the difference in saving animals, humans, and property. For our young people diagnosed with ASD, having them devise a plan not only provides them with confidence, but also creates a sense of safety and calm. This technique is quite simple. Each group member gets a piece of paper and a choice of marker or pen. The members are instructed to either write out their plan or draw it out, or both. The therapist gives prompts such as, "Think about where you are bullied the most;" "What adult is nearby that you can tell;" "Where is the nearest exit;" and, "What would you do if you were cornered in the bathroom?" These prompts help to get the members thinking of the various places and scenarios that they might be in when encountering a bully. The technique is helpful because the group can also discuss the various types of bullying—for instance, mental or emotional behavior that is used in cruel ways. Each member can devise a plan that mentally prepares him or her "in case" of an emergency. After each group member has written or drawn their plan, the plans can be discussed and sometimes this is a good brainstorming session for those group members that might be struggling with what to create for their escape plan.

Think Powerful and Think Smart!

The techniques discussed in chapter 4 of "Think Powerful" and "Think Smart" are important to also use with older children. Because older children tend to have greater thought abilities and capacity, it is important to introduce them to the power of positive, truth-based thinking. Due to the characteristics that many young people diagnosed with ASD possess, it is likely that they will encounter threatening behavior from others on their journey to adulthood. Equipping the young people with cognitive tools is essential in protecting their sense of value and worth.

Bullying Prevention in Group Therapy with Older Children: Emotional Tools

The true damage of bullying behavior is manifested in the emotional realm. Sadness, anger, frustration, and fear are spawned as a result of the experience of being threatened and hurt. A sense of hopelessness and helplessness become entrenched in the young person's psyche, cutting deep ravines and trenches in the thinking and feeling domains of the individual. A common thread in all therapy is equipping a person to understand and deal with negative emotions that he or she encounters in daily living. For individuals diagnosed with ASD, alexithymia creates major problems in both understanding and dealing with emotions; however, when the individual encounters bullying situations, the residual emotions can create great inner turmoil, resulting in self-loathing and destructive behaviors. Young people need tools to deal with negative emotions and maintain a healthy sense of self-worth and self-confidence. The techniques that follow will be helpful in providing older children with practical tools to process the emotional fallout that comes with bullying.

Comic Book Stories: "With Great Power, There Must Also Come Great Responsibility"

The above quote has resonated with comic book fans for generations. I have used this wonderful quote many times in my work with young people related to understanding and dealing with negative emotions. Born out of the comic *Spider-Man*, it helps to put into perspective the idea that no matter what a person feels, we must learn to control our behaviors and impulses in order to live well. When talking about comic books I also include Manga. Each superhero goes through a process whereby he or she must realize that the power they possess can be used for evil or good, and that unharnessed power is dangerous, as is the energy generated by negative emotions. I have found that many young people diagnosed with ASD, both boys and girls, enjoy comic books and Manga of all types. As I have become immersed in this world of art and literature, I have found wonderful parallels and metaphors to adapt the stories found in the books to the young person's real life, and more importantly, ways to teach them about overcoming negative emotions.

When it comes to bullying, there are countless metaphors found in comic books and Manga related to "bad guys" and the force of evil in general. In fact, what draws many children to the tales of the superheroes in these books is the fact that the hero represents someone stronger, smarter, and braver than the children feel themselves to be. The hero faces the bully or "bad guy," outsmarting them or destroying them, conquers evil, and saves the day. The group therapy setting is a wonderful place to discuss comic book and Manga characters and it is useful to begin by having group members discuss a favorite character from the comic book or Manga world. Keep in mind that for young people who do not read comic books or Manga, using a "hero" character from a computer/video game or movie is also acceptable. The next step is to identify how the group member's character expresses emotions and how the character deals with emotions. For example, when talking about anger, the Incredible Hulk comes to mind with his "Hulk Smash!" routine. The Hulk had to learn to channel his power, and there are countless examples of how he destroyed objects and almost himself before he learned to control his emotions and actions. Sayer (2007) discusses how Hulk is a good example of how memory and emotions become intertwined and that anger, along with the residual behaviors that stem from it, becomes hardwired into a child's brain. Offering alternative solutions and practicing those solutions are important in helping a child gain emotional control.

"I Get So Mad I Want to Smash Them!"

Adam, part of a group of older children, was discussing how being bullied made him very angry and "exasperated to the point of exploding." Like many young people diagnosed with ASD, he felt powerless to do anything in the presence of the bully, but at home Adam would rant and smash things when he thought of what happened during the day. He acknowledged that this led to him being put on restriction, but "it felt good to imagine smashing their face in!" Other group members commented that not only did Adam have to deal with the abuse of the bully from time to time at school, but that his release of anger only hurt himself in the end. One comic book character that Adam enjoyed was Batman, and we used the example of how Bruce Wayne, filled with anger, confusion, and fear over the death of his parents, turned his negative emotions inward and ultimately, suffered for it. He lived for a long time in seclusion, isolating himself from the rest of the world and was, in a way, "on restriction." When Bruce Wayne finally faced his fears, and learned to channel the negative emotions to positive places, he found the strength to develop skills that aided him in fighting evil. It was only then that he became Batman. The realization for Adam was a powerful one. He brought in one of his books that told the story of Bruce Wayne's transformation and together as a group we identified positive ways for Adam to deal with the anger that came from the bullying. He no longer took his anger out on himself at home. He began writing his own comic book story with himself as the main character; the character's main power was generating huge amounts of powerful energy that enabled him to help others and fight evil. He gradually found ways to confront the bully based on techniques described in other sections of the book.

Getting Rid of the Shame Game

A residual negative emotion that often arises from being bullied is shame. Stemming from thoughts related to believing one to be weak as well as being physically hurt and socially humiliated, shame grows like a diseased fungus and settles into a person's way of thinking and feeling. Shame keeps negative thoughts sprouting like mushrooms that give off toxic gases that form into more negative emotions such as worthlessness and hopelessness, leading individuals to live in fear and depression, and some end up taking their own life as a result. Children diagnosed with ASD often verbalize feeling ashamed as a result of being bullied, although many do not understand that there is a word that describes how they are feeling and have difficulty articulating the experience of feeling shame. I have incorporated a technique into my group therapy work with young people dealing with bullies that helps group members understand shame, where it comes from, and how to get rid of it.

The first part of the technique is to explain what shame is. I simply share that the feeling of shame related to bullying comes from knowing that something wrong was done to me and I either chose to do nothing about it or could not do anything about it. I explain that feelings of shame are sustained by negative beliefs such as "I am a coward," and "I am worthless." I also explain that the shame resulting from bullying is illusionary; the victim has done nothing wrong yet somehow feels responsible. Using a white board and marker, I write many of these types of thoughts on the white board. It is helpful if the group members can come up with their own personal negative thoughts related to shame, but keep in mind that for children, these concepts will be new and they may need some prompting or interpretation from the therapist to help put their negative thoughts into actual words.

I then show the group members how positive, truth-based thoughts do not contribute to the feeling of shame. For instance, when I think "I did nothing wrong; it is the bully who is in the wrong." When I think "I'm not going to let that happen to me again, I'm smarter now," the feelings of shame disappear. Using four or so white board erasers, I take the positive thoughts that group members formulate and put them on sticky notes and attach those to the backs of the erasers. Then, each group member takes one of the erasers and goes to the white board and rubs out one of the negative, irrational thoughts. After each group member has taken a turn, the white board is obviously clean and no more negative thoughts are seen. The visual picture for the group members is that because of the positive, truth-based thoughts, shame is gone.

This technique can be used with any negative emotion, and is a good way to introduce the concept of Cognitive-Behavioral Therapy (CBT) and Rational-Emotive Therapy (RET) to young people diagnosed with ASD. The technique also dovetails nicely with the mental and physical techniques used to deal with bullying behavior discussed earlier in the chapter. A behavioral component can be added to this technique in that group members can be shown how purposeful and intentional positive behavior such as standing up to a bully, telling someone about the bullying behavior, or refusing to be treated poorly, is helpful in reinforcing the positive truth-based thinking and further insulates that person against feeling shame. I find that young people diagnosed with ASD enjoy a visual representation of a concept and this technique provides a powerful reminder of how negative emotions can be "wiped away."

Chapter Six

Group Therapy with Adolescents Diagnosed with ASD

Adolescence is a time of great physiological, emotional, social, and cognitive turbulence. Adolescents experience many changes to their physical body, but also are bombarded by new emotional material as well as increased demands on their cognitive abilities. Socially, the adolescent is introduced to a complicated world and the expectations of adults continue to rise. Many adolescents realize that in a few short years, they will be "on their own" which adds pressure in the form of deciding upon a career and if they will attend college. Academically, many adolescents experience a greater workload with advanced classes. Many adolescents experience a change in the home environment, due to parents' increased expectations and shifting family dynamics that often occur during a young person's adolescent years. Due to the minefield of rapidly shifting physiological, emotional, social, and cognitive factors, many adolescents display odd behavior that baffles parents, teachers, and caregivers. I often remind parents of a quote by Josselyn (1954), which sums up the behavior and thinking of the adolescent quite nicely:

> The behavior of the adolescent is typical of that of individuals, of whatever age, who have not found an adequate integrative pattern with which to reconcile their own impulses, demands of conscience, and the demands of reality. Adolescence, as is equally true of neurosis and psychosis, is characterized by relative failure of the ego. Demands placed upon it have caused a strain that it cannot meet. (p. 225)

Thus, to paraphrase, the demands outweigh the resources.

For adolescents diagnosed with ASD, all the above challenges must be faced; however, this must be done with the additional burden of the developmental difficulties that carry over from childhood. Many parents mistakenly believe that their child will "grow out of" the difficulties that ASD brings. However, while the form of the challenges may change, usually those challenges follow the child into adolescence, and the possibility exists that things may get worse. For example, many adolescents diagnosed with ASD experience real depression for the first time as a result of the increased social rejection. Since the young person's ability to think and reason has usually increased, he or she uses this new reasoning to simply turn negatively inward, blaming themselves for the rejection and thinking "I must be the problem." Also problematic for the adolescent diagnosed with ASD is the confusion regarding emotions and the inability to interpret the emotions of others. Due to the complexity of new social situations and the increased pressure of society to "fit in," the adolescent diagnosed with ASD often experiences greater frustration, anger, and sadness, and so on, but making matters worse, has no idea what to do with the emotions or how to combat them. Add to this the difficulty that individuals diagnosed with ASD have with putting thoughts and feelings into words, and it is no wonder why so many young people diagnosed with ASD are stricken with depression and anxiety, and many contemplate suicide.

Group therapy with young people diagnosed with ASD can be a powerful force in not only helping the young person overcome the challenges of ASD, but to offer these remarkable individuals hope and light—hope in the form of seeing that the future offers them good things, and light in the form of learning to find the beauty and gifts inside themselves. One of the great joys in my work is helping young people see that adolescence does not have to be a time of gloom; there are miracles all around us if we choose to look for them. While adolescence can be frightening, it is also a wonderful time that can be enjoyed. I believe we as therapists working with adolescents play important roles in being cheerleaders for them on their journey to adulthood, in addition to being a trusted guide. The following techniques are designed for the therapist who works with adolescents diagnosed with ASD in helping them understand and deal with negative emotions, create a sense of self-worth and self-confidence, increase the young person's perspective-taking skills, teach skills to learn to build and sustain relationships, and to provide tools to deal with bullying behavior.

GROUP THERAPY APPLIED TO EMOTIONAL ISSUES OF ADOLESCENTS ON THE AUTISM SPECTRUM

Adolescents diagnosed with ASD need help with understanding emotions and learning to interpret the emotions of others. Understanding what emotions are and being able to tolerate negative emotions such as sadness, fear, and frustration are a necessary part of development. Those who do not learn to tolerate these negative emotions tend to become reactive, which leads to poor behavior choices. Many young people diagnosed with ASD are overcome with fear at the thought of approaching adulthood, which drives many into isolation (Hull, 2011). Parents of adolescents diagnosed with ASD often feel trapped when it comes to helping their young person move to a new stage of responsibility and joining society. On the one hand, the parent does not want to cause more emotional damage by forcing the young person to do something that terrifies them, like learning to drive or get a job, but on the other hand, the parent feels guilt that he or she is somehow enabling the adolescent, and many are frustrated by the feeling they cannot help their young person overcome fear.

Learning to interpret the emotions of others is an important foundation of building and sustaining relationships. Being able to identify when another person is sad, frustrated, bored, and so forth is essential in navigating the social world. Individuals diagnosed with ASD usually struggle with this, which leads many others to perceive them to be indifferent, rude, and lacking empathy. This is not true; in fact, individuals diagnosed with ASD, while being affected by alexithymia, care deeply for others but have difficulty showing it and putting these thoughts and feelings into words (Bird, Silani, Brindley, White, Frith, & Singer, 2010). Many adolescents with whom I work tell me that they want friends and desperately want to connect with others, but they do not know how. Many share their feelings of sadness and frustration over not having friends to talk with and spend time with. I am saddened and angered when I hear of people's misconceptions that people diagnosed with ASD are "robots" and "anti-social"; some of the most compassionate and kind people that I have ever met are on the autism spectrum. The great challenge for the therapist is to help the individual diagnosed with ASD to learn to recognize emotions in others and accurately interpret those emotions. While this is no easy task, I believe the group therapy setting provides an excellent setting to teach young people this valuable skill. Because most adolescents have more advanced cognitive skill than children, they tend to understand more complex concepts and ideas, which aids the therapist in his or her effort to help the young person gain a greater understanding of emotions and recognizing and interpreting the emotions of others.

Recognizing Emotions in Others: Using Forms of Media to Recognize and Understand Emotions

Human beings expressing emotion is a common part of movies, television shows, and other forms of media such as video and computer games. In fact, many times the emotions expressed in these forms of media are exaggerated;

people who are angry in a television show are *very* angry, those that are excited in a movie tend to be *very* excited, and so on. Actors usually perform to great dramatic effect in these forms of media. I have found these forms of media to be a helpful tool in getting young people to learn to identify emotions in other people for several reasons. First, most young people, especially adolescents diagnosed with ASD, have a particular television show or movie that is dear to them. In fact, one of the most common questions that I ask young people is, "What type of movie do you like," or, "What do you like to watch on TV?" and usually I find at least one show or movie that the young person is interested in. Once the movie or show is identified, I can begin to dissect it with the young person and find out what it is about and who the main characters are. Second, most young people identify strongly with the characters in the show, movie, or video game. Because these are characters that the young person has spent a great deal of time watching and getting to "know," he or she understands the personality characteristics of the character. Third, by observing the character or characters with the young person diagnosed with ASD, the therapist has an opportunity to ascertain the level of emotional awareness that the young person has, and the therapist can point out various emotions that are expressed. This technique contains rich material to use in helping young people recognize emotions as every show or movie will contain interactions between characters complete with accompanying emotions.

I find that many young people diagnosed with ASD are actually quite good at identifying emotions of a certain character in a movie or TV show, but struggle to do so with "real" people. I am not sure why, but it seems to be common. However, regardless of the reason, I find it encouraging that the connection to a TV show or movie provides an excellent avenue to help the young person identify emotions in people he or she comes in contact with on a daily basis. The group technique begins simply by asking the members what TV shows or movies they enjoy and describing the characters that are a part of those. Often, there will be commonalities among the responses—for example, two or three group members may enjoy a certain Japanese anime show. The next step is to find video clips of the shows or movies and view them as a group. I recommend that the therapist review some of the clips ahead of time, in order to have specific emotions he or she can show the group, and also to make sure that the material is not offensive. I try to make connections between the material in the show or movie and common situations that may happen in group members' lives. For example, while *Star Wars* is completely fictional, Han Solo being extremely annoyed with Chewbacca's shenanigans is a common, everyday occurrence that could really happen. Also, even though no one can actually master the elements like Ang in "Avatar," it is evident from the joy on his face that when he does so he is doing something he really enjoys. The focus of the technique is getting the group members to identify the emotion in another person and understand the "why" of the emotion. This part of the technique is done through going around the group and asking each member to identify a particular emotion that the character or characters are displaying. Once this is done, the discussion can be expanded to have the group members identify a situation in which they noticed that identical emotion in another person in their personal life, whether at school, home, or some other setting. It is important for the therapist to remember when using this technique that every individual diagnosed with ASD is different when it comes to his or her ability to recognize emotions. Just as neurotypical individuals differ in levels of social awareness and abilities, so do individuals diagnosed with ASD. Once a particular emotion is identified, the therapist can ask the group members follow-up questions such as "Why do you think the character is feeling bored when this person is talking?" or "Why is this person annoyed when this person asked him to change seats?" These questions serve to get the group members thinking about more advanced social situations with complex emotional content and to give them practice in identifying those emotions.

Avatar: The Last Air Bender—A Path to Increasing Emotional Recognition and Understanding

I used the above technique with a group of adolescents to whom I was teaching the skill of recognizing emotions. Two of the group members enjoyed the show "Avatar: The Last Air Bender," and while other two members did not watch the show, they knew about it and were interested in the story. I was familiar with the show and found several clips of the characters in various situations in which many different emotions were displayed. The show revolves around three main characters: Ang, the "chosen one" who will be the next great "avatar," and Katara and Sokka, a brother and sister duo from the "water tribe." Along the way, other characters are introduced and the group finds themselves in funny, serious, and even life-threatening situations in which they must work together and overcome personal fears in order to save the world from the evil "fire nation." The group often argues and jokes with each other, and then, when danger appears on the horizon, bands together and uses each of their individual strengths to move through the catastrophe and towards safety. This particular show was helpful because the characters are in the teen range and many of the exchanges between characters are similar to everyday experiences. I honed in on the exchanges between the characters, and found several different displays of emotion. For example, Katara was usually the calm, level-headed member of the group, while Sokka, her brother, tended to be immature and egotistical. Ang, although naïve and boyish, had a sage-like wisdom that would both impress his friends on one hand and make them laugh on the other. I picked three- to five-minute clips of the friends in various scenarios and asked each group member to identify the emotion that he or she saw exhibited. Following this, we as a group would discuss how one could tell what someone was feeling from their facial expressions or tone of voice. The character of Sokka, who is often sarcastic, was very helpful in helping the group members understand and recognize sarcasm, something with which individuals diagnosed with ASD often struggle. Feelings of boredom, sadness, grief, and many others were evidenced through this show and this technique provided a valuable tool in teaching the group members to recognize and understand emotions in others.

Putting Feelings into Words

Adolescents in general, whether neurotypical or diagnosed with ASD, struggle with putting feelings into words. As young people near adulthood, relationships become more complex and it is important for a person to be able to voice what he or she is feeling in order to build and sustain relationships. For individuals diagnosed with ASD, this ability often proves difficult due to the challenges of alexithymia, and as a result the individual often experiences relationship difficulties as others perceive him or her to be uncaring and lacking empathy. The group therapy process can provide valuable tools for young people diagnosed with ASD to learn the skill of verbalizing emotions. For this technique, I simply use a white board and marker and write an emotion at the top of the board. I then have the group brainstorm various descriptions of the emotion in order to see what ideas the group formulates. This part of the technique stems from my belief that it is wrong to assume that an individual diagnosed with ASD is deficient when it comes to expressing emotions; each group member should be approached with respect and from a strength-based approach. I have often been surprised at what a group member knows or can do and it always benefits the group experience when this happens.

Once the emotion has been written down, I write a few phrases or prompts underneath the emotion. For example, if the emotion is "sadness," I will write "I am feeling sad. I feel sad when______. When I'm sad, I need people to ______." These simple phrases or prompts allow each group member to see that putting emotions into words is a simple process, and that by keeping it simple, one can avoid becoming overwhelmed or paralyzed as many of these individuals often feel when asked what they are thinking and feeling. These phrases can be modified or added to if need be, depending on the various characteristics of the group members and depending on their circumstances. For example, one young man in my group lived with his grandmother who had raised him from the time he was about five. He had resorted to yelling at her when he was annoyed, because of the difficulty he had in explaining his feelings. She then would become hurt which left him feeling terrible, and he did not know what else to do. For him, one of his prompts was "Grandma, I'm feeling annoyed. This means I'm frustrated. Please give me some space and then we can talk." Another young man in the group, being raised by his single mother, was experiencing the same type of issue, and this prompt helped him as well. The goal of the exercise is to simply get the group members to practice identifying what emotion they are feeling and then putting into words what they are feeling and what they need from another person in that situation.

GROUP THERAPY APPLIED TO INCREASING PERSPECTIVE-TAKING IN ADOLESCENTS ON THE AUTISM SPECTRUM

Perspective-taking is important in all phases of life, but adolescence marks an especially important time because of the rapidly shifting emotional, social, and physiological landscapes that are common during this time of development. Discouragement that begins in early adolescence as a result of feeling rejected and ignored can quickly take hold and form deep roots of despair that create social problems that carry over into adult life (Rao, Beidel, & Murray, 2008). Increasing the perspective-taking ability of an adolescent diagnosed with ASD is important not only for social development, but also for the young person's sense of self-worth. A healthy sense of self-worth is important in the adolescent years, as it is a time of many milestones like learning to drive, job seeking, and preparing to leave home. The group therapy setting is valuable for increasing perspective-taking in adolescents diagnosed with ASD. One reason is that many young people are naturally seeking out social relationships at this age. Despite the fact that individuals diagnosed with ASD struggle with forming relationships, the desire for connection and relationship is alive and well. The individual simply does not know how to begin forming a friendship, but holds a deep desire to have a friend. I find in my groups with adolescents there is a hunger to connect with others and this creates a context for the perspective-taking work. The second reason is that the young person is more mature and has developed greater physical, cognitive, and emotional abilities. Thus, when techniques designed to increase perspective-taking are introduced, there is a developmental foundation for the information to be understood and subsequently put into practice. A final reason that group therapy is valuable in helping to increase perspective-taking is that the group is a place of safety, which creates the opportunity for emotional growth and learning to occur. It is impossible to learn when one is in "fight-or-flight" mode, and young people on the autism spectrum are easily triggered into this mode, especially in social situations. The group therapy setting represents a social setting that is safe, relaxed, and a fun environment, and the skills that are learned in the group therapy setting can be generalized to larger social situations.

The following techniques are designed to help the adolescent learn to increase his or her ability to "read" the thoughts and intentions of others and see situations from another person's perspective. When one reads literature on the subject, it can seem as though this is a nearly impossible task. And yet, I find that with a solid therapeutic relationship, and in a group environment that is warm and accepting, gains can be made in this area. My work with individuals diagnosed with ASD has taught me to always bring a dash of hope and optimism with me wherever I go, for we do not fully ever know the far-reaching effects our work will have with these remarkable young people.

Video/Computer Games

I have discussed the use of video/computer games in helping to increase perspective-taking with children, and now I will present how useful these games can be with adolescents diagnosed with ASD. The draw of adolescents to video/computer games is almost universal, and introducing video/computer games to adolescents in the group therapy setting usually brings reactions of pleasant surprise amongst group members. There are several variations of using video/computer games in group therapy with adolescents to increase perspective-taking. One way is to allow each group member to share his or her favorite game, and to teach the other group members how to play it. This "show and tell" type of sharing not only puts the presenter in a leadership/teaching role, which helps to increase confidence and self-worth, as well as social skills, but creates an opportunity for the presenter to have to think like his or her audience in order to teach them about the game. I usually have a laptop or gaming console set up, and I always invite group members to bring their own. Depending on the length of the group, it may be helpful to only allow one group member to share per session, in order to give adequate time for the explanation of the game and to allow group members to play it. Another way to introduce the game is by watching YouTube videos of actual game play, which can be helpful if the therapist does not have the specific type of gaming console available.

Virtually any video/computer game can be used in teaching perspective-taking. The therapist can formulate a list of questions prior to beginning game play to get group members thinking about what the player (or character) is thinking and feeling. Examples of these would be:

1. Imagine being the player right now. What would you do differently?
2. What do you think the player is feeling right now?
3. What do you think the character might be thinking/feeling right now?

Pausing the action and getting the group members to comment on the action is helpful to prompt discussion and refocus members on the task at hand.

One game that I have found to be very useful is the Sims game series, manufactured for a number of various consoles and platforms. The Sims have been reported by therapists to be useful with children and adolescents (Fanning and Brighton, 2007) as a play therapy tool (Skigen, 2008) and specifically, with those diagnosed with ASD (Hull, 2011). The uniqueness of the Sims game is that the players create a representation of themselves, complete with "personality, marital history, and job skills" (Hull, 2011, p. 107). The player builds a house and acquires possessions, and must get a job in order to pay bills and pay for entertainment. What is most helpful from a therapeutic standpoint is that the player has the opportunity to interact with other players, or "sims" and can choose from a number of responses to questions, or the player can initiate conversation. Relationships can be formed, such as friendships and dating, and players can get married and have children. I have found that adolescents, both neurotypical and those diagnosed with ASD like to play the Sims game, and it is a useful tool in teaching social skills and more specifically, perspective-taking.

The Sims game can be used in group therapy either with single-player or multi-player modes. The therapist can use the game to teach perspective-taking through the modeling of various emotions, like happiness or anger, based on the responses of the character in the game the player manipulates. The therapist has the opportunity to pause game play and prompt group members to consider the motivations of the player's character as well as the other characters in the game in order to observe the interactions of others. This can lead to discussion of possible options for each player ("When you asked the girl for a date, she became angry and walked away. Perhaps it was because you had just met her and there was no friendship established first. Asking someone for a date when you have just met them might make them uncomfortable.") Scenarios such as these can be repeated, but with a more appropriate response and then the subsequent action occurs (The character does accept the invitation for a date). The most important factor in using a computer/video game, whether the Sims or other type of game, is the therapist uses the scenarios within the game to emphasize the thoughts and feelings of the characters in the game and the players, and to get group members to practice imagining being in another person's "shoes."

TV Shows and Movies

TV shows and movies are full of verbal and non-verbal interactions between characters, and also contain moments in which solitary characters are shown to be thinking and feeling various thoughts and emotions. The movie "Castaway" for instance, starring Tom Hanks, has nearly an hour of footage in which the main character is marooned on an island and the audience is left to speculate what the character is thinking and feeling, simply by observing the behavior of the character. The character begins a relationship with a volleyball he affectionately names "Wilson," talking to the ball from time to time and gleaning a sense of companionship and hope from the inanimate object. I have used clips from this movie in particular, to get group members to imagine being in such a predicament and to explore the various thoughts and feelings that might be experienced. It is important to remember that there is no "right" or "wrong" when gathering thoughts and feelings of group members; the goal is simply to get group members to practice being in another's "shoes."

I recommend the therapist use a number of different clips from TV shows or movies so a broad range of interactions and scenarios can be viewed, and it helps to use shows the group members are familiar with and enjoy. However, it is also useful to throw in material that group members are completely unfamiliar with as well, because this helps to resemble what social situations are like for those diagnosed with ASD. I have learned the hard way that only using material group members like can reinforce specified interests and keep the individual "stuck" in his or her development. Individuals diagnosed with ASD can sometimes appear offended at having to watch a show or movie with which they are unfamiliar, stating loudly, "This is boring!" The therapist should gently but firmly remind the group members if this happens that life sometimes has elements that we all find a bit boring, or isn't necessarily our "style," but that relationships are about learning new things and sharing in new experiences. One young man who attended a therapy group I ran was quite vocal at having to listen to or watch something he did not like, immediately dismissing it as "boring" and "stupid." He was very resistant and at one point I had to take him outside the group therapy room to calm him down. I would not be deterred by his tantrums, and I continued to gently but firmly insist on his tolerance of others. Through consistent exposure to music, TV shows, and movies that he did not like, this young man gradually learned to tolerate others' preferences, and this generalized to being able to listen to others' opinions as well. Over time, he was able to keep his outbursts to himself and provide a more socially acceptable response, even though he would tell me privately he strongly disliked another group member's preference of movies or TV shows.

Did this young man magically learn perspective-taking? Can I say that his ability to read the thoughts and feelings of others greatly increased through group therapy? I cannot say for sure, but there was improvement in two things. One, this young man learned that other people have different tastes than he in movies and TV shows, which, while shocking to him, was instrumental in him learning to tolerate the unpleasant emotions that came with watching something he did not find interesting. Second, his exposure to these various feelings and thoughts and being able to tolerate them, provided a foundation for future social relationships through learning socially acceptable responses and shifting his perspective about others' opinions and preferences. I bring this up because it is easy to become discouraged when working with individuals diagnosed with ASD because at times the therapist may feel as though he or she is not making a difference or that group members are not "getting it." However, the therapist must remember that through consistent exposure and practice of skills, as well as having a sense of optimism and encouragement, change can and will occur. It is important to fight off discouragement and not give up!

Thought-Bubble Training

Thought-bubble training, discussed in chapter 5, is an effective technique that can be used to teach perspective-taking skills to adolescents diagnosed with ASD. The technique is done the same way as described with older children in chapter 5. Because adolescents tend to be a bit more advanced on the developmental ladder, this technique can be both fun and enlightening. I have noticed that adolescents tend to give more information than children do, and because adolescents are in more complex social situations, the responses can be quite varied. The therapist's role in using this technique is to assess the group members' abilities to read another person's thoughts and feelings, and then to teach the group members based on the scenarios. I have also tailored this approach to use scenarios that group members have told me about, such as interactions at school, or with their family members at home. This technique can be a fun way to teach perspective-taking, and provides the therapist with yet another tool to teach this valuable skill.

GROUP THERAPY APPLIED TO INCREASING SELF-WORTH AND SELF-AWARENESS FOR ADOLESCENTS ON THE AUTISM SPECTRUM

Perhaps at no other time in a human's development is self-worth and self-awareness both so necessary and yet, often, so lacking, as during the period of adolescence. Neurotypical adolescents, as well as those diagnosed with ASD, are often severely depleted of a sense of self-worth and self-awareness, as the explosion of growth in every area of the human body creates emotional and cognitive chaos. For adolescents diagnosed with ASD, there is extra chaos as the difficulties already present created by autism cause confusion for the adolescent and sometimes rejection by their peers. A healthy sense of self-worth and self-awareness is necessary for any young person getting ready to enter adulthood, but even more important for those on the autism spectrum. For those diagnosed with ASD, the challenges experienced in adolescence tend to follow them into adulthood (Rao et al., 2008) and create a great deal of problems. Group therapy can be beneficial in helping to increase self-worth and self-awareness in adolescents diagnosed with ASD for several reasons.

First, while the time of adolescence can be chaotic, I find these young people are hungry for someone to listen to them and also to guide them, and many prove to be eager learners when it comes to building up their sense of self-worth. Much like the old proverb which says that the most helped wayfarer is the one who recognizes he is lost, young people often enjoy the therapy experience because they find it to be a place in which they are is listened to and respected. The group therapy setting, complete with a therapist who provides a warm and accepting environment, along with comrades who are like fellow soldiers marching into battle, is a wonderful place in which to find comfort, compassion, and understanding. Also, many find it a fun enterprise to become more self-aware, and this self-realization often comes with the pleasantness of being surprised at learning more about themselves, and what makes them "tick." Second, the group therapy setting is often viewed as a safe place, which creates the fertile mental and emotional ground in which self-awareness can be taught and the young person's sense of self-worth can be built up. Third and last, the other "players" in the group therapy experience can provide a boost to a young person's sense of self-worth in ways that a solitary therapist never could. The comments of other group members, such as "Yes, that is an excellent painting—you really are talented," or, "Wow, you play the guitar so well—that is really cool . . . I wish I could. Can you show me how?" provide a wonderful backdrop of encouragement and genuine praise that is a powerful way to help a young person see himself or herself as having value and worth.

Self-Worth Exercises

I use a variety of techniques in helping to raise the self-worth of adolescents in group therapy. One quick and easy way is to simply have the group members come up with a list of their talents: that is, things that they believe they are good at. The therapist simply provides a legal pad and pen and a prompt, such as "I am good at . . ." and then allows group members to write down whatever comes to mind. This exercise gets the young person to step back and look at himself, examining and assessing a personal inventory of gifts and talents. The therapist should be prepared, however, for the possibility that young people diagnosed with ASD may not write anything down. For example, when I first began doing groups with this population, I conducted this exercise and was surprised that after three minutes or so none of the group members had written anything. "You can't think of *anything* that you think you are good at?" I asked, leaning forward with a quizzical look on my face. I reassured them that none of them had to say it out loud if he or she did not want to; I waited, and still, nothing. Then I changed the prompt to "What do I like to do?" and that generated more responses. From those responses, I then had the group members assess their gifts and talents related to activities they enjoyed as opposed to simply asking about their talents. For example, a young man who enjoyed computers was able to admit he was good at understanding and working with computers, but the thought never occurred to him until he focused on the first fact, which was "I enjoy working with computers." I found it was easier for the young people to generate a response to the first question from this angle for some reason. I have never come across any formal research regarding this, but I have noticed the same trend in neurotypical adolescents as well. Perhaps it is simply because of the universal feelings of identity confusion that give all adolescents a touch of unawareness, or perhaps it is the general feeling of inferiority that many adolescents experience. Regardless, this technique is a good way to help young people see their abilities and learn to value those abilities. If a group member either chooses to not participate or after much prompting has nothing written, I simply give them my thoughts regarding what I think their gifts and talents are and leave it at that. Sometimes, young people are so self-conscious that they do not want any attention at all drawn to themselves and we as therapists must be sensitive to such things so as not to make things worse.

A variation to this technique is to have group members assess each other's talents and gifts. This technique is especially useful with an established group in which members are familiar with one another. Each group member's name is written on a piece of paper with space provided underneath the name for members to come up with talents and gifts that they perceive their group members possess. This exercise can also help with perspective-taking through having group members concentrate on each other and shifting their angle of awareness. This exercise can be quite powerful and I am often surprised, as are group members, by the keen awareness of their peers. One young man I remember glowed with pride when he realized that his fellow group members noticed his great knowledge of nature and history and actually valued his opinion. I honestly believe that I witnessed an increase in his sense of self-worth in that very moment, and this remained intact throughout the duration of the time I worked with him. As with any technique, a time of discussion to assess group members' thoughts and feelings is useful in order to answer questions and clarify the purpose of the technique.

The "Show and Tell" technique discussed in previous chapters is another way to allow the value and worth of an individual to shine. Group members bring in items or are allowed to talk about their specified interest or passion and by doing so are able to feel a sense of value and worth. It is my belief that no matter how old one becomes, there is a universal desire to share what someone loves. For adolescents diagnosed with ASD, their specified interests can be broad, from video/computer games and technological gadgetry to sewing, knitting, or gem collecting. One young lady in our group would sing and play the guitar, in addition to sharing all sorts of different musical styles and tastes, which educated the rest of us and celebrated her gifts and talents.

Personality: A Pathway to Self-Awareness and Developing an Awareness of Others

I once had a psychologist tell me that if there was one gift he could give to the world, it would be to administer a personality test to each human being along with a detailed summary. We were discussing the struggle of humanity in general and failure of marriages and relationships in general, and he told me he believed it was due to a general lack of self-awareness in human beings. "People don't know who they are or what they want" he said. A lack of self-awareness leads to poor decisions in choosing careers and mates but also negatively affects everyday relationships and influences negative patterns of self-soothing such as alcoholism and drug abuse. This conversation, held years ago, never left me and it led me to formulate a single uniform goal for every person, whether parent, child, adolescent, husband, or wife that entered my office: that each person would have an understanding of who he or she is and what it is they want out of life.

Nothing has brought me more joy over the years than helping people better understand their personality and to understand the people with whom they live and work. This understanding is never to judge, hurt, or dominate another person, but simply to find pathways to better communication and to find awareness as to the "why" of conflict and misunderstandings. Feelings of anger and revenge are often replaced with feelings of understanding and empathy when people discover that the behavior of another, previously perceived as a personal attack, is actually due to that person's personality and previous negative life experiences. A colleague of mine, Dr. Frank Schultz, says that every behavior a person exhibits has to do with love and safety: If I don't feel loved and I don't feel safe, I am likely to lash out or withdraw from others. When I perceive that I am loved and feel safe, I can stay relaxed, be in the moment and form relationships (Schultz, 2005).

I do not employ formal testing tools but choose rather to keep things simple, as I will attempt to do here in this section. Because I work primarily with young people, I found that formal tests were too complicated. Instead, I provide a broad overview of the four personality types and use characters with which young people are familiar, such as characters from TV, movies, or books, to demonstrate those personality types in everyday people. Since most adolescents barely have a handle on who they are or what they want, I find simple is best. The group therapy approach is one in which I describe the four personality types. Sanguine, the constantly happy and sociable personality, can be described through the characters of Sponge Bob, Tigger from *Winnie the Pooh*, and Sid from the movie *Ice Age*. Choleric, the passionate and serious leader personality type can be seen in the characters of Wolverine, Master Tigress from the movie *Kung-Fu Panda*, and the Joker from *Batman*. The Melancholy personality type, characterized by careful and thoughtful actions and serious thinking, can be seen in Eeyore from *Winnie the Pooh*, and Dr. Gregory House from the show *House, M.D.* The Phlegmatic personality, characterized by being passive and kind, a "peacemaker" of sorts, can be seen in the NBA basketball player Tim Duncan, Winnie the Pooh, and St. Thomas Aquinas.

The personality types and corresponding characters can be given to group members typed out on a piece of paper, but I prefer to write them one at a time on a white board and discuss them. This is helpful to get group members to identify characters they might be familiar with from a favorite TV show or book series, or someone that they know such as a family member or peer. Once explained, I ask each group member which personality type he or she thinks describes them best, and I remind each group member that the goal is not to label or be put "in a box" but simply to understand themselves better, and also to learn about others through learning the various personality types. I also take some time to explain how some types can clash, especially when a high-energy person comes in contact with a low-energy person—for example, when Tigger runs over Pooh and does not seem to notice. It is helpful for the therapist to talk about their personality type, and also to disclose the various personalities of others that his or her personality type both fits and clashes with, in order to get discussion going. The therapist should remember this information is probably new to group members of this age; however, I usually find that once I offer up a character from a TV show, movie, or book, there is a good deal of identification and an increase in understanding.

A final part of this technique involves helping group members use their new knowledge of personality to work through conflicts with others. For example, many of the adolescents with whom I work have conflict with siblings. I use part of the group session to have group members identify their family members' personalities, especially siblings. Quite often, the personality of the group member is opposite in many ways to the sibling with whom there is conflict, and interestingly, those who are close to siblings often have like personalities, or at least large areas in which their personality styles overlap. This is very helpful in not only self-awareness, but also in helping to increase the perspective-taking ability of the group members, and also is helpful for teaching the group members ways in which conflict can be minimized at home with their siblings.

Tommy's Revelation: "My Sister Isn't a Jerk!"

Tommy, a fifteen-year-old group member diagnosed with ASD, constantly talked about his younger sister and how she was "annoying." Things had escalated to the point between them that their mother approached me about family counseling to help them learn to get along. Following the group sessions in which we discussed personality types, Tommy had a revelation. He remembered vividly the *Winnie the Pooh* cartoons from when he was younger and instantly identified himself as "Eeyore" and remarked that his aunt had actually called him "Eeyore" when he was young. As he was becoming older, he also saw himself as a little bit like House from the show *House, M.D.* as he was close to one or two people and had little patience for other people's "frivolous" mannerisms. He identified his younger sister as "Tigger"—bouncy, happy, and "dangerously positive." When we mapped out the conflicts between them, Tommy quickly identified that he was most annoyed when she "pounced": that is, like Tigger, showing up unannounced and surprising him with some new toy, gadget, or YouTube video that he cared nothing about. This actually frightened him and created an urge inside him to want to yell or lash out at her physically, which he had done in the past. He assumed that she planned these ambushes, waiting for him behind a wall, or planning the attack in a pre-meditated "ninja-like" style. Following the personality training, however, he was shocked to discover that this was "how she was wired" and I can still see the look of shock and amazement as he said to the group, "She isn't a jerk!" From this revelation, Tommy was able to scale back his reactivity as a result of the increase in his perspective-taking. The conflict between him and his sister nearly ceased, and Tommy was able to verbalize his frustration instead of yelling or hitting.

Adolescents and Bullying: Group Therapy Techniques

I have written extensively about bullying in chapters 4 and 5, and there is little doubt about the extensive bullying that adolescents diagnosed with ASD experience on a daily basis. Many of the young people I see in my office, both individually and in group settings, recount verbal, emotional, and sometimes physical attacks from others. The effects of the bullying are far-reaching, from emotional and mental scarring to extreme social withdrawal and deep self-loathing. As a therapist who cares deeply for these remarkable young people, it is hard at times to listen to these stories. While society seems barely concerned about the bullying of children, it is even less so regarding the bullying that goes on during the adolescent years, especially when it relates to those diagnosed with ASD. Our culture seems to believe that bullying is a natural part of adolescence, and I am witness to the deep scars and wounds that are left behind in the hearts and minds of the young people with whom I work. The process of working with adolescents diagnosed with ASD who are bullied is much the same as what I discussed in previous chapters regarding children and bullying. The therapist must empower the young person mentally and emotionally, and because so many adolescents have been bullied severely, the therapist must be able to help with healing the wounds that have already occurred. The techniques discussed in the previous two chapters are also able to be used with adolescents; however, there are two I want to include specifically in this section because of greater emotional and mental maturity that adolescents typically possess. The first is a narrative approach and the second involves the power of drama to help a young person heal and grow.

Putting Feelings into Words: A Narrative Approach

Adolescents in general struggle with putting feelings into words, but especially those diagnosed with ASD. A hallmark trait of ASD tends to be the difficulty the individual has in translating emotions into words so others can understand. When a traumatic event such as bullying occurs, the "fight-or-flight" responses of the sympathetic nervous system limit the brain's ability to form words and give meaning to the event, leaving the person in a state of emotional disequilibrium. For young people diagnosed with ASD, this is even more agonizing as the images, sounds, and emotions become locked even deeper inside them, creating an inner turmoil of stress and self-loathing. Helping young people diagnosed with ASD put feelings into words, especially those who have suffered bullying, is very important. Narrative therapy is based on the idea that the individual can reconstruct the troubling situation or event as he or she wishes, and see the problem from a different angle. Cashin, Browne, Bradbury, and Mulder (2013) state, "Narrative therapy is aimed at surfacing alternate ways of seeing problems and how the person is positioned in relation to the problem which in turn influences their ability to move forward in a less-distressed way (p. 33). Narrative therapy is an effective tool to use with adolescents diagnosed with ASD and who are struggling with bullying because it allows the therapist and group members to isolate one part of the problem, describe it, and formulate solutions to the problem. Individuals diagnosed with ASD tend to take in problems as "chunks" of information, instead of as a sequence of events, which can lead to great amounts of distress and confusion (Cashin, 2008). As a result of looking at the problem from a different angle as a result of the narrative approach, the young person is able to alleviate stress and also learns coping skills for future problems (Cashin et al., 2013).

Narrative therapy begins with an understanding of the young person and how he or she views the problem. I view this stage of the process as a "brainstorming" session in which the problem is described, feelings and thoughts are noted, and sometimes a name is given by the adolescent to describe the situation or their reaction to it. For example, a young man who was very passive when being bullied, but who experienced huge amounts of destructive anger later when he was home alone, described this phenomenon as the "blasting zone" because this was the time when he would lash out and smash things that were dear to him. Each group member is given the task of writing out these "triggers" and descriptions in order to promote a sense of self-awareness as well as seeing the problem from a different point of view. One young man pretended he was a newspaper reporter on assignment writing about a boy (himself) who allowed himself to be taunted by a bully and called it the "Jerk Update." This helped him view his passiveness from a comfortable distance and instead of feeling guilty and shamed, it helped him come up with strategies for standing up to the bully. I also allow group members to draw out the scenarios and write small captions about what is going on, as some adolescents diagnosed with ASD find writing to be very tedious and an unpleasant experience. For group members who are very resistant, I use my laptop computer to type out the situation and the various thoughts and feelings of the group member and print it out for them.

The next phase of narrative therapy is to have the group members keep a journal in which they track the daily progress of the situations and monitor their thoughts and feelings about the event. Keep in mind that for some individuals diagnosed with ASD, this will be difficult; however, I work with neurotypical adolescents who are just as resistant regarding this part of the work. The goal is that the work begun in the group session generalizes to the young person's personal life so he or she gains greater coping skills and problem-solving skills in dealing with new or challenging situations. During the next few group sessions, the journals can be reviewed and discussed and new coping skills can be identified or the problem can be re-examined based on the insight of the young person. The group dynamic creates the benefit of support, offers different perspectives, and encourages group members to believe in themselves and an attitude of "I am not alone" in facing the problem of bullying.

The last phase of narrative therapy is the creation of a story that takes the problem, solutions, and alternative actions and combines them into a chronicle of an alternative reality that leads the young person towards healing, empowerment, and overcoming the challenge. The story belongs to the individual, and no matter how ridiculous it may be to me, far-fetched in its imaginariness and dream-like state, I must not judge it as ridiculous, and must discourage other group members from doing so as well. The story is where the power lies in narrative therapy; it is the golden nugget that comes from the prior digging and sifting through the problem, identifying thoughts and feelings, and coming up with alternative solutions. It is the story that brings it all together for the young person; the chronicle is the spark that lights the burner of empowerment that translates into positive, intentional behavior and emotional control. Cashin and others (2013) noted that narrative therapy was helpful in increasing levels of hope in young people, which translates into a greater sense of self-worth and less fear.

John's Story

John, a fourteen-year-old male diagnosed with ASD, attended group therapy twice a month. When first introduced to narrative therapy, John was completely resistant. He hated writing, and while he possessed a very high intelligence, he saw it as tedious and boring. He loved movies, however, and dramatic storylines found in manga and video games. John had been bullied severely in his early middle school years, and while it only happened occasionally now, he would become explosive when it did, lashing out at fellow students and teachers. He had voiced how he hated being "at the mercy" of such strong feelings, and he recognized that being able to control the emotions would help him, but he had no idea how. He carried great amounts of anger when he thought about past bullying experiences, mainly that he "did nothing about it." Now that he was physically, mentally, and emotionally more mature, he found himself wracked with guilt and self-loathing at the thought of doing nothing when bigger classmates tormented him.

When I first introduced the concept of narrative work with John's group, the other members eagerly accepted it, except John. Like many adolescents, the thought of writing out thoughts and feelings brought back unpleasant experiences in school, and the last thing I ever want to do is make the group therapy experience like school. However, I felt that there was a great deal of benefit in using this approach with this group, especially John. He had experienced a great deal of physical growth in the past year, putting on at least fifty pounds and had grown almost six inches. He had figured out that he could be quite intimidating physically, and like a superhero who usually nearly self-destructs until their power is harnessed, John was getting into trouble at school and at home because of not being able to control his emotions and behavior reactions. I believed if John could view the issue of his emotions and unpleasant memories from a different perspective, it could lead to greater self-control, which could translate into a greater sense of self-worth and more positive social experiences. John voiced the desire for relationships, but had developed a pattern of pushing people away. John even pushed away his fellow group members, whom he had known for over a year. When given a compliment, John would "playfully" throw something at the person who had given the compliment, or push the person. When John would open up occasionally and become vulnerable during a group session, he would follow this with hurling insults at his fellow group members, including me.

Like I often do with resistant young people, I was able to find an alternative to John's hatred of writing. John liked to draw and was a fan of manga, so we compromised by agreeing that he did not have to write anything as long as he could draw out a scenario or a picture that represented his thoughts and feelings. I also informed him he did not have to write out full sentences, a few descriptive words were all that were necessary. One element that helped John was that his fellow group members, who also had been bullied and struggled to put their experience into words, came up with phrases and metaphors for their experiences. The support of his peers helped him find descriptive words that he could not previously articulate and encouraged him in the process. John finally was able to come up with a name for his story. He called it "Deconstructing John." He explained that this name was a metaphor for how he, like a robot with defective parts, needed to be taken apart and the damaged parts that needed replacing taken out, and the various wires and circuits that were either frayed or not making connections needed to be mended. His drawings showed a robot, at times out of control, with sparks and parts flying off of it, in various stages of causing destruction. One of the captions simply said, "He is out of control!"

The next phase of the narrative therapy centered around coming up with solutions to the problem. The group setting dynamic creates a wonderful combination of encouragement and ideas for overcoming challenges. Often, what one person is going through, another person has already encountered, and thus can offer a different perspective and alternative solutions. John was shocked to hear that other group members also had broken things at home out of anger over an incident at school, and many of the items were something near and dear to them that left them with feelings of guilt and shame. These sessions were powerful and productive, and I could see that John's sense of self-worth and self-control were improving because he was listening to the group members and was taking their suggestions to heart. When it came time to continue the story, John actually wrote some of it, along with the drawings. The robot was getting worked on and underneath was a paragraph that explained the various pieces that needed to be replaced. One of these items John called the "Anger Amplifier," a metaphor for a device that took a small amount of anger and magnified it many times. It seemed that this device could be useful when someone needed to defend themselves in a life-threatening situation, but was detrimental because there was no way to control it. The robot needed an "Anger Over-ride Switch," which John explained as something that could take the extra anger and safely channel it out of the body, sort of like a breaker in an electric box. The explanation of the devices paralleled my explanation to the group members of how, when a person becomes angry, the sympathetic nervous system ("fight-or-flight") response engages, which is useful if someone is in a life-threatening situation. However, most of the time, it simply causes problems as people become reactive, like John, saying and doing things that are out of control. I was pleased because it showed me that he was paying attention to my explanation and that he understood it. We discussed what an "Over-ride Switch" would do in real life and came up with several techniques that John could employ to help himself self-soothe. One of the most important things was that John learned to recognize the signs within his body that would tell him he was getting increasingly upset. He came up with the term "Sweat Sensor" and added it to the list of items that would be put inside the robot. He shared with the group that he noticed when he was starting to get upset, he would sweat, mainly on his palms and forehead. He realized that his palms and forehead getting sweaty would be his signal to begin his list of self-soothing techniques.

The last phase of the narrative therapy in the group setting is crafting a story in which the problem is overcome. I am always intrigued by the plots and outcomes of these stories. Some of them could be written as screenplays and become major motion pictures. Some involve magical occurrences and mythical creatures; others, like John's, involve technology and machinery. John's final version of his story was one in which the robot (John) finally is able to control his anger, and to my surprise, the extra energy that is left over is not simply for the robot's self-interest, but to help others. The robot realized it was wasting energy by causing all this destruction and people did not like this version of the robot. However, the robot realized that by helping others and becoming a friend, not only did the anger disappear, but there were friendships to be made. I was truly touched by this part of the story and I was stunned by John's revelation; this insight was something that he discovered through the art of narrative therapy and while I acted as guide, I was powerless to instill this insight into John. He had to come upon it himself.

Getting Dramatic: The Power of Acting Out Traumatic Events

Drama therapy is a powerful way to instill social skills as well as increasing perspective-taking and problem solving to help young people overcome challenges (Tricomi & Gallo-Lopez, 2012). Group therapy is a wonderful setting to "get dramatic" as there are other people present to take on various roles and create ideas. There are many ways to use drama, from traditional role-play to the use of puppets or figures; from play and script writing to the use of visual arts. The use of drama helps young people form greater understanding of themselves as well as others, and helps instill a greater sense of self-confidence through role-playing various roles, or roles that seem daunting. For example, one of the groups I conduct with adolescents has members who are getting to the age of finding a part-time job. For many of these young people, ordering food at a restaurant can seem frightening, so the process of getting a job is extremely anxiety provoking. However, in the group therapy setting, I set up a role-play situation in which the adolescents act out the process of going to an interview, and experience the process of seeking employment. While the group therapy setting is not as real as going to an actual job site, the exercise is productive on two levels. First, through practicing the role of interviewing for a job, the individual learns interviewing skills. Second, the fear that comes from doing something the young person has never done before is lessened somewhat because there has been at least some exposure to the event through the role-play.

The use of drama is productive in helping a young person overcome trauma, such as that which comes from a bullying experience. Due to the difficulties that young people diagnosed with ASD have with putting thoughts and feelings into words, dramatic interpretation offers them an effective way to communicate about their fears and find solutions to the problem. Much like narrative therapy, the use of drama allows a young person to look at the situation from a different perspective which can improve coping and provide the young person with a sense of hope. Similar to narrative therapy, the beginning phases of drama work involve getting group members to share their experiences and to look for common themes. For example, fear of being bullied again, a sense of helplessness, and shame and guilt over not doing anything are three common emotional themes in adolescents who have experienced bullying.

The next phase involves "warming up" which is a time of getting the body ready to be spontaneous and free, and is helpful to pull young people diagnosed with ASD out of repetitive and rigid thought and behavior patterns. This phase involves games, such as passing a ball around or mirroring, an exercise that involves two group members pairing together and following each other's movements in a leader/follower format. The idea is to help the young people move out of their typical roles that they are in most of the time, and to enter a space that is free and spontaneous. Tricomi and Gallo-Lopez (2012) also recommend space walking and the freeze game. Space walking involves participants pretending to be in different situations such as walking in a strong wind or floating in space. The freeze game is described as "asking participants to move freely and then to quickly freeze" (p. 277). The therapist asks the participants to explain what they are doing at the time of being frozen, such as interacting with another person or animal, or playing a sport.

Gallo-Lopez is the founder of the All Community Theater (ACT) Project which works with children and adolescents diagnosed with ASD through the use of the ACT© method, developed by Gallo-Lopez and Tricomi in order to "develop social skills and relationship-building, improve communication and relatedness, and enhance spontaneity and creativity" (Tricomi & Gallo-Lopez, 2012, p. 278). While I am not a registered drama therapist, I have found that incorporating drama into group therapy can be a wonderful way to help adolescents deal with the traumatic effects of bullying and build coping skills through telling the story and working through the problem. After the "warm-up" phase, there is a period of story building through gathering ideas and putting together the "who, what, when, and where" that are common elements of any story. The goal is to get group members to think about their personal experiences and to prepare to share the information with others. This is useful in creating an important link for the individual diagnosed with ASD who tends to internalize every thought and feeling. Practicing organizing the story helps to create a context of meaning concerning the event, and helps form a narrative that will be told by the individual.

Group members may need help getting started, especially those that are not familiar with the exercise. I often use the format of a storyboard, similar to what a movie director would use to show group members how to put ideas together. Similar to the brainstorming phase in narrative therapy, some may be more comfortable with drawing out scenarios as opposed to writing, and the therapist can help the group member identify important thoughts and feelings. Once this is complete, it is time to begin the show! I often ask for a volunteer that would like to be the "director" and use the other group members to bring his or her script or storyboard to life. The "director" identifies who the main characters will be and then instructs them as to what roles they will be playing. For example, Sarah, acting as the director, will explain to Jeremy and Adam that Adam is being bullied by Jeremy. Adam is to stand up to Jeremy and tell him that he cannot bully him any longer. Rachel, another group member, will play the role of a school principal who is going to be walking up just as Adam is telling Jeremy that he cannot bully him. As one can see from this example, the process of acting out the story places group members in various positions. Jeremy, a passive person by nature, has never bullied anyone, but has been bullied himself. Playing the role of the bully can help him shift perspectives and connect with the bully's insecurities or need to dominate. Adam may be acting out standing up for himself for the first time in his life. Sarah, a very passive individual, yet who loves theater, is allowed the chance to be in charge of her story, which can increase her sense of self-worth and allows her to practice being assertive. Rachel, playing the role of the principal, is allowed to experience life from the perspective of a leader who is responsible for situations like this that happen every day. Group members can also use puppets, props, and costumes in the process of acting out the story.

Once the story is acted out, there is time for debriefing and "de-roling" (Tricomi & Gallo-Lopez, 2012, p. 281), a term that describes how the actors pull out of the roles that they are playing and return to "real" life. This time of discussion allows group members to share their thoughts and feelings regarding being in the roles that they played, and positive and negative reactions to being in the roles. At times, there will be powerful emotional reactions from playing a certain role, and the therapist plays a "coaching" role to help group members put feelings into words. The therapist should always monitor for those group members who appear to be getting emotionally overwhelmed during the experience, and the debriefing time is helpful to work through these emotions. Group members may be confused by feelings that surfaced during the exercise, and it is important to allow questions to be asked regarding certain roles.

I am always surprised at the effectiveness of this approach and how much discussion is generated following the role-play sessions. The technique is also helpful to instill perspective-taking as well as helping to instill a greater sense of self-confidence in young people diagnosed with ASD. The technique is valuable in giving young people diagnosed with ASD the opportunity to use a range of emotions while role-playing, such as humor through practicing joking. I have observed a great deal of improvement in coping skills as a result of this approach. As young people play a different role, it helps them achieve distance from the problem and instills a sense of safety so that coping skills can be identified. This technique is one more way to help young people feel empowered and gain valuable experience in dealing with difficult situations like bullying.

Chapter Seven

Group Therapy with Adults Diagnosed with ASD

Adults diagnosed with ASD struggle with the same developmental issues as children and adolescents but experience greater pressure from society and family members to be independent and self-supporting. The general belief in most cultures is that once children become adults, they will be able to join society and either find work or go to college, after which there will be a career established and independent living will naturally occur. For people with special needs, such as ASD, this most certainly is not the norm, as many of these individuals must rely on family members and community supports in order to survive. Much of the literature and media attention regarding ASD focuses on children, and most of the resources available are geared towards school-age children and adolescents. As more and more children and adolescents are diagnosed with ASD, it is certain that there will be more and more autistic adults entering society and attempting to find a place to fit. Today, many adults diagnosed with ASD must rely on parental and family support, and many of these family units are headed by single mothers who do not have great financial resources or knowledge of community resources.

I have been in practice long enough to see many of the clients who came to me as children move into adolescence and finally reach adulthood. For the young people diagnosed with ASD, this is one of the greatest honors of my life as I witness them taking steps towards adulthood and then stepping into college or the workforce. While this is a miracle of sorts, I am saddened as I observe the organizations that provided valuable services to these individuals while they were children and adolescents, no longer offer services now that the individual is an adult. Many continue to come to me for the mental and emotional support on an individual therapy basis and I am happy to serve them, but I witness the bleakness of what many face when they reach adult age: very few transition services, hardly any social groups, and few opportunities to begin independent living. For those who struggled academically, college is not an option; for many diagnosed with ASD, the demands of a trade education are too much and the thought of working a full-time job is completely overwhelming. Because many diagnosed with ASD have co-existing challenges like ADHD, learning disabilities, and processing disorders, their career choices are severely limited and many will not make enough money to live on their own without family or government assistance.

CLINICAL CONSIDERATIONS REGARDING GROUP THERAPY

Due to adults diagnosed with ASD being such a unique population with varying cognitive, emotional, social, and family characteristics, some clinical considerations are necessary. I draw heavily from the work of Yalom (2005) in this section as I believe that it serves the therapist well to examine some cautions as well as exciting possibilities when working with these amazing individuals. I review some of the factors that were discussed in the beginning of the book, but I do so with adults diagnosed with ASD in mind. Therapy, especially group therapy, with individuals diagnosed with ASD is a unique experience and the therapist must be prepared to be unprepared to a certain degree. What I mean is that, while formal training and research is no doubt important, there remains an element of the therapy process, especially with a unique population like those diagnosed with ASD in which there will be unexplored areas. The therapist will be left to discover these unknown lands with the clients, and what will be discovered is simply the beautiful truth of connecting in human experience and relationship in order to learn, heal, and grow. Yalom (2005) addresses the matter well when he says, "Therapist effectiveness has much to do with the capacity to improvise as the context demands it, drawing on both new knowledge and accrued wisdom. Manuals on psychotherapy do not provide that" (p. 562). For therapists who are going to work with individuals diagnosed with ASD, these words ring especially true.

Addressing Varying Developmental Levels

The word "spectrum" used to describe those with autism is certainly apt. Individuals diagnosed with ASD are very different and I remark often I have never met two that are just alike in personality, gifts and talents, and challenges of daily living. While the traits of those on the spectrum are shared, the ways in which the traits are manifested are always different. For example, while two individuals may struggle with building relationships, one may be very verbal and talk incessantly, which pushes people away; the other may be completely silent, not knowing what to say and appearing paralyzed, which also turns people off. Two people on the spectrum may exhibit an obsession with specified interests; one is able to turn his into a career and find a place in society in which he fits, while the other's unique interest is something that keeps him alienated from society. These differences in personality and characteristics create a wonderful tapestry of distinction, but there is often confusion by family members and novice therapists that "if I've met one, I've met them all." This notion is not true and has been further cultivated by the media; *Rain Man* for instance, presents a picture to the world of "this is what a person with autism is like." This notion raises people's expectations and serves to stereotype those diagnosed with ASD. For example, when people find out I work with those on the autism spectrum, some well-meaning but very misinformed people will remark, "I saw a thing on *20-20* about that; they are the people that are geniuses and invent all sorts of things, right? Are *your* people all millionaires too? This guy was; I mean he was like . . . *Rain Man*." I do my very best to use the next minute and a half to educate the person, but as soon as I use the words "not typical" and "normal intelligence" the person usually loses interest and wanders away, seeking more stimulating conversation. Many diagnosed with ASD do have a higher intelligence, but many are of average intelligence. Just like a sampling of the neighbors in the neighborhood, you will find varying interests, abilities, and preferences.

Developmentally, individuals diagnosed with ASD fall on a very wide continuum. While individuals diagnosed with ASD share many developmental challenges, how those challenges manifest themselves in the person's life is very different. While some individuals may be able to work full-time jobs, find a life partner, and raise children, many cannot, which goes against much of society's assessment of what is "normal." Another complicating factor is that the developmental challenges of the individual diagnosed with ASD are not observable to the naked eye. I often hear people remark, "I didn't know he was autistic; I mean, he looks so *normal*." While this may sound insensitive, many people, especially neurotypical individuals who have not been exposed to individuals on the autism spectrum, are left to assume that autistic individuals have physically identifiable characteristics. When it comes to helping an adult diagnosed with ASD seeking employment, it is advisable for those with more severe challenges to have family members assist the adult diagnosed with ASD locate career assessments and vocational testing in order to make the individual and caregivers aware of the various challenges as well as gifts and talents the individual possesses.

The therapist who wishes to conduct group therapy with adults diagnosed with ASD must take into account all of these issues so that each individual's needs are understood, and the group is tailored to meet those needs. Yalom (1995) recommends screening group members so that the group is of utmost benefit to the individual and that there is a right "fit" for the individual seeking group therapy. The therapist must do his or her due diligence to find out the various needs of the prospective group member, as well as abilities to ensure that the group experience is as helpful as possible to the group member. Clinical information, interviews with the prospective group member, as well as input from family members can help the group therapist tailor a group approach that is beneficial. Because of the various needs of individuals diagnosed with ASD, inquiring of the expectations of the group member not only promote a sense of respect, but also safety. Many prospective group members may have never had a group therapy experience and do not know what to expect. Informed consent is of utmost importance.

Setting Flexible Group Goals

The setting of group goals is an important part prior to starting a group. The therapist must have an idea of what he or she is hoping to accomplish and what the focus of the group will be. For example, is the group going to focus on helping group members overcome emotional issues, such as depression and anxiety? Or, will the focus be on improving social relationships through social skills training? I have found that many diagnosed with ASD are so starved for contact with others, they are happy just to find a place to talk with someone who accepts them. By examining the goals the therapist wishes to accomplish, group members can be presented with a clear presentation of the purpose of the group. Sometimes, the group will evolve as the various needs of the group members become apparent. One group with young adults I conducted was originally begun to help group members improve social skills, but it quickly evolved to helping the members overcome fear, deal with negative thinking, and improve the sense of self-worth of the group members. While social skills continued to be part of the focus of the group, the cognitive and emotional issues of the members took center stage as it became apparent that those issues were more pressing at the time. The therapist must be ready to shift the focus of the group to meet the needs of members, but still maintain a focus on the original goals of the group.

Safety

A sense of safety is important to all human beings, and is necessary for the human being to be able to learn, grow, and connect successfully with others. I have written in earlier chapters how individuals diagnosed with ASD easily enter a state of "fight-or-flight" and get stuck in that state, a phenomenon which hampers the individual's ability to deal with the stress of daily living and interact socially with others. The group experience likely will, at least initially, trigger emotional arousal as the group member is entering a new situation and meeting new people for the first time. This can be anxiety provoking for neurotypical individuals; however, it must be remembered that for the individual with ASD, engaging in a new experience like group therapy and meeting new people may be very overwhelming. The therapist must remember this and work hard to create an environment that is warm, accepting, and with the least amount of "triggers" as possible.

The subject of fears and anxiety-provoking triggers are good items to inquire about during the screening process so the therapist is aware of what may activate a person's "fight-or-flight" response. For example, a group member may be extremely sensitive to various sounds, especially loud sounds. Some may be triggered by the dynamics of the room, such as the squeaking of a chair on a tile floor. This information not only helps the therapist eliminate as many triggers as possible prior to the group experience, but can also give meaning and understanding as to a particular group member's behavior during group. While it is impossible to anticipate and eliminate every possible trigger, the preliminary effort by the therapist will yield great gains in both building cohesion in the group and helping to instill a sense of safety for each group member.

Concurrent Group and Individual Therapy

Clients often become part of a therapy group due to the urging of their individual therapists, and some may begin individual therapy following attendance of group therapy sessions that encourage the individual to explore issues in the more intimate setting that individual therapy provides. Many of the members who attend my groups are also individual clients, and the group therapy sessions serve as a working stage on which the skills gained during the individual sessions are showcased, and vice versa. Yalom (2005) states that seeing a client in individual and group therapy can be "an exceptionally productive and powerful therapeutic format" (p. 435). One major benefit is that clients are less likely to drop out of therapy when attending both group and individual sessions. Another benefit is the therapist has the advantage of tailoring the group sessions for the client's benefit as a result of the knowledge gained in the individual sessions. For example, knowing that my client whom I see in individual therapy has just made a huge breakthrough with an issue that is being discussed in group therapy, offers an opportunity for that client to share his success and be a help to the other group members.

However, there are some issues for which a therapist who acts as both individual and group therapist must be ready. One issue is that of boundaries. The therapist must clearly define his or her role with the client as an individual therapist and group therapist. Clients often want reassurance that the group therapist is going to uphold confidentiality and not betray them in the group format. Certainly, this can create problems if the therapist is not careful in this area, and he or she must reassure the client that confidentiality will be honored. A second issue that can arise is that the role of the therapist becomes blurred when attempting to keep the world of individual therapy and group therapy separate. A therapist, especially a novice therapist, may forget what was shared in an individual session and bring it up in the group session, causing the client distress. A final issue that may arise is the client who wishes to talk about other group members in individual therapy. The therapist must remember boundaries and be able to keep the worlds separate, and if this occurs to direct the client to bring the issue up in the group therapy environment (Yalom, 2005).

GROUP THERAPY AND EMOTIONS: TOOLS AND TECHNIQUES FOR ADULTS ON THE AUTISM SPECTRUM

Individuals diagnosed with ASD often struggle with emotions. I have discussed the difficulties related to alexithymia and how many individuals diagnosed with ASD can easily become overwhelmed by emotions. While battling negative emotions is a common experience for all humans, those diagnosed with ASD are affected on deeper levels because of the characteristics of autism. These characteristics create major problems for adults on the autism spectrum in forming and sustaining relationships, and achieving independence due to the effects of stress and fear. Group therapy for adults diagnosed with ASD can be helpful in learning to cope with stress because it provides the individual with peer support and association with others who are struggling with the same issues. Group therapy also provides a warm, accepting environment in which the tools that are taught can be practiced and fine-tuned within the safety of the group.

Adults diagnosed with ASD often experience great amounts of stress because of increased financial, career, and social pressure. Another source of stress can be the loss of a familiar routine or place. For example, when a young person graduates from school or can no longer participate in a program because of reaching adult age, the individual can often feel a sense of loss as well as stress that comes from having to establish a new routine. A key theme of adult living, especially in the early stages, is going to new places and meeting new people which can be difficult for individuals diagnosed with ASD. Stress is debilitating for all humans, but for people diagnosed with ASD, it is especially crippling. Many individuals diagnosed with ASD do not have good coping tools with which to deal with stress, and as a result tend to either shut down or lash out. Group therapy can help adults diagnosed with ASD learn to cope with stress through teaching the individual to self-soothe, and teaching members to channel the energy generated by stress towards positive outlets, such as thinking positive thoughts and engaging in intentional and productive behavior.

Teaching Group Members to Self-Soothe

Learning to self-soothe is a valuable part of successful adult living. Stress can never be totally eradicated, and the demands of daily living constantly present individuals with obstacles and challenges that must be overcome. I have explained in earlier chapters how stress triggers the "fight-or-flight" response, which puts the brain in "survival" mode. As a result, the individual becomes more reactive, as the parts of the brain that control emotional and behavioral impulses are less available due to the activation of the sympathetic nervous system. Self-soothing can be achieved through a simple exercise that involves relaxing the stomach muscles. A colleague of mine, Dr. Frank Schultz, shares an exercise in his book *A Language of the Heart* (Schultz, 2005) that details how one can turn off the "fight-or-flight" system and achieve a non-reactive presence. The exercise involves relaxing the core muscles of the lower stomach. It begins with taking a deep breath and then releasing the air slowly. As the air is released, the individual simply allows their stomach muscles to "unclench," which will allow the belly to go soft. When the individual keeps the belly soft, a shift will occur in the muscles of the body resulting in the individual feeling "blob-like." Most individuals will experience their shoulders immediately dropping and often they report feeling "heavier." The reason for this is quite simple. When the stomach muscles are released, it is impossible for tension to be held anywhere in the body. Once the tension is released, the "fight-or-flight" (sympathetic nervous system) system is turned off as the threat of danger is no longer detected and thus the activation of the sympathetic nervous system is no longer necessary. Without a detection of a threat, the body gradually switches over to the parasympathetic state, the normal state of the body when it is calm and relaxed. When the body switches over from sympathetic to parasympathetic state, the frontal lobe of the brain comes back "online." The frontal lobe controls the logic/reasoning and decision-making ability and is less accessible when the individual is stressed (Hull, 2012; Schultz, 2005).

This exercise can easily be taught and practiced with group members. I find that teaching this valuable exercise to group members early in the group therapy process provides them with a valuable tool that can be used immediately outside of group but also within the group experience as new skills are taught and emotional content arises. For example, certain topics that are discussed during the group experience may trigger intense emotional reactions, and when the therapist notices this happening, he or she can direct the group member to implement the non-anxious presence. The exercise is valuable with group members who experience debilitating levels of anxiety, both during group and outside of group. Learning to achieve a non-anxious presence gives group members a practical tool that can be immediately implemented in their everyday lives no matter what situation they encounter.

Relaxation Techniques

Along with the non-anxious presence, relaxation techniques are useful to give to group members to help them cope with stress and anxiety. The group therapist should have a wide knowledge of simple techniques that can be taught to group members to assist them in improving their daily living through the elimination of stress and fear. Because those diagnosed with ASD are easily triggered by environmental and social factors, having a "toolbox" of skills and techniques will be valuable. I am a proponent of giving clients skills and tools to lessen and eliminate fear and stress so that learning and growth may occur. For adults diagnosed with ASD, fear and stress can be crippling as the individual attempts to find their way in a world that seems to offer very little to those who need assistance. Breathing techniques, journaling about the triggers and cause of fear and stress, positive imagery, and yoga are just a few of the techniques that clients can learn to eliminate and lessen the effects of fear and stress and gain control of their environment.

Brian and Overcoming Fear and Stress

Brian, a young adult diagnosed with ASD, began attending group therapy sessions when he mentioned to his individual therapist that he was interested in meeting other young adults like himself and to work on forming relationships in a small, safe setting. Brian struggled with great amounts of fear, and in recent months had been feeling "very stressed" due to the fact that he needed to find a job in addition to making decisions regarding a career and whether or not he would attend technical school or community college. These decisions created fear in Brian because he felt as though he was a burden to his aging grandfather, with whom Brian lived, and he felt pressure to become self-sufficient. The individual sessions with Brian focused on helping him learn to self-soothe and to channel his stress towards positive outlets, such as applying for jobs or researching potential careers and trade schools. One of Brian's triggers was meeting new people in new social situations. Joining the group provided a good place to put his skills learned in individual sessions to good use.

Brian was very nervous prior to the group session, but took his seat and watched as the other group members filed in. Brian was relieved that the group session began with a time of relaxation. He already knew the technique and soon found himself joining in the conversation and while he was a bit anxious when it was time for introductions he was able to use his self-soothing techniques and did very well. He was surprised at the kindness of the group members and how they accepted him. Over time, Brian began to enjoy the group sessions and they proved useful in helping him grow and learn to become more comfortable in social situations. From this experience Brian gained a great deal of confidence in his ability to enter social situations. In just a few months, he had found a part-time job and was taking classes at the local vocational school.

Recognizing and Identifying Emotions in Others

I discussed earlier how individuals diagnosed with ASD struggle with alexithymia, which is known as the inability to recognize the emotions of others and to interpret one's own emotions. For adults diagnosed with ASD who are entering more complex social situations such as going to college, technical/trade school, and beginning careers, the ability to recognize and interpret the emotions of others is very important in forming relationships and navigating these complex social situations. For example, I worked with one young man who worked as a waiter in a restaurant. He shared with me that his supervisor was very happy with his performance of his duties, but there had been some complaints by some of the patrons. Apparently, the patrons had attempted to joke with the young man, but he, being very conscientious of doing a good job, did not understand the humor. Confused, he simply ignored the comments of the patrons and went about his work. The patrons interpreted his behavior as "rude" and "dismissive." The young man and I discussed ways in which he could better learn to understand if a person was joking or not.

The above story represents a common experience for those diagnosed with ASD as they enter more complicated social situations. Thankfully, this young man had a supervisor who cared about him and knew of his challenges related to ASD. Many diagnosed with ASD are not as lucky and many find themselves being fired or not considered for promotions because of being misunderstood. Group therapy is useful in helping adults learn to recognize emotions in others. The first technique to help adults diagnosed with ASD learn to recognize and identify emotions in others is through Thought-Bubble Training. This technique is done in much the same way as the technique discussed in the chapter for children and adolescents. The therapist uses a white board or large pieces of paper in which a scenario is presented and then the group members can identify what the character is thinking and then attempt to judge the various emotions once they have identified the thought. The therapist can then lead the group in discussion of what emotions have been identified and guiding group members to an accurate assessment of the emotions. A second technique is through the use of TV and movie clips that demonstrate people in various social situations. I have found this technique is useful to help adults diagnosed with ASD identify and recognize sarcasm, something with which individuals diagnosed with ASD often struggle. This technique is used in the same way that was described in chapter 6, with group discussion of the various emotions that were identified in the clips. The therapist must do his or her homework with this technique, finding scenes from TV shows and movies that group members can relate to and also contain the themes with which group members struggle.

Expressing Emotions: A Narrative Approach

Individuals diagnosed with ASD often struggle with expressing emotions. Due to the complications of alexithymia, the individual struggles to put the feelings into words. Group therapy offers the individual diagnosed with ASD an opportunity to learn to understand his or her emotions and put them into words. Narrative therapy is a good way to introduce the concept of relating feelings. Many people, whether neurotypical or on the autism spectrum, struggle with putting feelings into words. Through the use of narrative therapy, adults diagnosed with ASD can learn to express their feelings and as a result, form and strengthen relationships. The technique is similar to what was discussed in chapter 6; however, when working with adults, it is important to expand the topic base to include settings such as the workplace, meeting new people, and doing things for the first time. The technique begins with gathering ideas regarding the various situations that create struggles and challenges for the individual group members. For example, one group member of a group I conducted was very excited to have found a job working in a hospital, but found that one element of the job he did not anticipate was talking to people. One thing people commonly asked him was "How are you doing?" This question confused him, and he often sat paralyzed, confused as to how he should answer. I wrote this scenario out on the white board and began to map out possible answers the young man could give, and then the group members helped him identify what he was feeling. One woman shared with him how when she was asked such a question would think, "What is the answer I'm supposed to give?" and "What is a feeling I might be feeling right now that would be safe for me to say?" This helped the young man immensely and is an example of how using narrative therapy in the group setting adds to the power of the technique because of the input of other group members.

Once these struggles and challenges are identified for each member, then the "brainstorming" part of the technique is done as the individual and group members work to find solutions to the problem. This working phase of therapy can be very exciting as group members realize they are not alone in their struggle and they are cared for by others as demonstrated by the group's help in finding solutions. Members are instructed to write down the solutions on legal pads so they can review those for later. This phase of the technique involves the "homework" of journaling and putting the solutions into practice. The final phase of the therapy is writing a story that involves seeing the problem from a different angle. For the young man mentioned above, the narrative approach helped him see the problem from a different angle, and because he could see different outcomes, he no longer feared the situation.

He was able to write a short scenario that involved him giving several different responses and carrying on a conversation with people, instead of being paralyzed. He mentioned the technique helped him to actually stop and think about what he was feeling, and through this practice he was able to connect with various emotions and put them into words. Narrative therapy is useful with a variety of issues, and is a valuable technique when working with adults diagnosed with ASD.

RELATIONSHIP-BUILDING TECHNIQUES FOR ADULTS DIAGNOSED WITH ASD

Learning to form relationships is an important part of adult living. Many adults diagnosed with ASD that I meet express an interest in forming close relationships with others, and many report feeling lonely. Most simply do not know how to get started. Group therapy is effective in helping adults diagnosed with ASD learn to build relationships and serves as a stage on which the relationship skills gained can be practiced. One reason why group therapy is so effective in helping group members learn to build relationships is because of the opportunity for those diagnosed with ASD to meet others who are similar in mannerisms and world view. I have heard more than one group member remark, "I didn't know there were other people like me." Many individuals diagnosed with ASD live in isolation from people other than family members and the group therapy environment can provide rich interaction with others who share the same life experiences. It is easy to see life from only one perspective, especially when one leads a solitary life. Through interaction with others, group members experience a natural shift in perspective by hearing how others see the world and experience it.

Another reason why the group therapy setting can help adults diagnosed with ASD learn to form relationships is that specific skills can be taught to group members. Learning how to start a conversation, using specified interests, learning to improve perspective-taking, and overcoming the fear of rejection are all skills that can be learned in group therapy. Perhaps the greatest advantage of teaching these skills in the group therapy setting is that the skills can be practiced immediately with the other group members, with whom there exists a sense of trust and safety. This presents a disadvantage for the individual therapist, who often struggles to find a practical setting for the individual client to practice newly acquired skills in a real-life setting. The practice of these skills is necessary to help build a sense of confidence and to help overcome fear and insecurity. I remind my group members that all human beings, neurotypical and those on the autism spectrum alike, have to learn social skills at some point in their developmental journey. In addition, everyone has to practice those skills to become adept at interacting with others. I find that this provides a sense of comfort and encouragement to group members, who often assume neurotypical individuals are born with the ability to navigate social situations smoothly.

Conversation: It's Sort of like Ping-Pong

Conversation is a foundational component of interaction between humans. When considering the elements of beginning conversation, it is important to remember the importance of context. For example, when helping the young man I mentioned earlier who worked in a restaurant, it helped to show him that in the context of a restaurant, people are not expecting deep conversation. Most people are simply expecting a short response of agreement or a brief explanation of one's place of birth, for example, due to the transient nature of interaction. Once the young man realized this, he felt relieved and was able to memorize a few appropriate responses to the questions or comments that were typically made by customers. I help group members realize the importance of context, and that much of conversation between human beings is shallow. Two people sitting at a bar, for example, sharing a space for an hour or so, are going to discuss career history, family history, and hobbies such as sports or some other activity. Once a friendship is formed and there is more interaction between people, the conversations tend to evolve into deeper areas such as thoughts and feelings about personal matters. It is important when helping group members diagnosed with ASD understand the elements of conversation that the concept of the context of a conversation be addressed.

To help group members understand the dynamics of conversation, I use the visual representation of a game of Ping-Pong. Ping-Pong, a variation of tennis, has the back and forth motion of a typical conversation. One person serves a greeting, for instance, and the other person returns a response, which can then be followed up with another question or a pause, waiting to see if the initiator of the conversation will ask a clarifying question. Sometimes, the topic of a conversation ends. At this point, just like in Ping-Pong or tennis, a player can "serve" up another topic through a comment or question. These "serve" topics can be comments about the weather, sporting event, or a current event going on in the local, national, or world context. I share with group members that once a conversation is going, it takes little effort to keep it going. Using the visual aid of the game of Ping-Pong or tennis has proven helpful as group members share how this picture helps them when starting and sustaining conversation.

Specified Interests: A Potential Relationship Builder

Individuals diagnosed with ASD are notorious for their unique specified interests. Many of my group members are interested in such things as sports, nature, technical gadgets, and video games just to name a few. I often use the individual's specified interest as a way to learn to form relationships with others. For example, one young man who was a wrestling fan and who was eager to make friends found that connecting to others online through wrestling sites led to meetings at local restaurants to watch matches that were broadcast on a weekly basis. Some of these connections led to deeper friendships that were formed around the young man's specified interest. I often encourage group members to seek out group meetings related to their specified interest and to join them. For instance, one group member who was passionate about photography found a group that met twice a month at a local church. He not only found an outlet to share his interest and passion, but was able to make new friends as well. This encouraged him and was instrumental in him starting his own photography business.

Role-Play: Practicing the Art of Forming Relationships

I have discussed the usefulness of role-play in previous chapters. Role-play can be used with adults diagnosed with ASD and is effective in helping group members practice the various skills mentioned above. Group members can practice making conversation, talking about difficult topics, or practicing comforting another person. Group members can be divided into pairs or groups of three while the rest of the group members observe the role-play. A time of discussion and feedback is important for group members to ask questions or offer comments to those who just finished the role-play. The power of this technique is twofold: The members participating in the role-play are practicing the techniques in real time and the other members who are observing are learning through watching the mannerisms of their fellow group members. I have found the feedback sessions are valuable as group members provide encouragement to those involved in the role-play as well as help with improving perspective-taking. While criticism is welcome and helpful, the therapist must be sure each group member understands that group members' comments are intended to help and not harm. The therapist may need to step in should the comments of other group members become harsh or if the role-play participant becomes upset by the comments.

Field Trips

One of the benefits of working with adults diagnosed with ASD is the therapist has freedom to conduct group sessions in places other than the therapy office. For example, the group may meet at a bowling alley, restaurant, or mall, in order to put social skills into practice. Meeting together outside of the traditional meeting place can be helpful in the following ways. First, this gives the group members an opportunity to practice newly acquired skills in real-life settings. Second, the camaraderie the group provides can give group members a great sense of confidence to overcome fears and insecurities. For group members who are particularly shy, even ordering food at a restaurant can be an anxiety-triggering experience. However, knowing that he or she is in the situation surrounded by fellow group members who have proven to be trustworthy friends can help the individual feel empowered. The therapist can also use field trips to build greater cohesion in the group through the members needing to depend on each other due to being in a new place. Field trips can also be centered on an individual's specified interest, which can help with increasing the individual's sense of self-worth.

WHO AM I, AND WHO ARE YOU? HELPING ADULTS DIAGNOSED WITH ASD UNDERSTAND PERSONALITY

I discussed the importance of helping individuals understand personality in chapter 6. For adults diagnosed with ASD, understanding personality is very important in self-awareness and learning to form relationships with others. Many people, both neurotypical and those on the autism spectrum, are not aware of their personality characteristics and how their personality affects relationships with other people. I discussed earlier how those diagnosed with ASD have different personalities and despite the characteristics that individuals on the autism spectrum share, all have a distinctly different way that they show themselves to the world through their personality. I discussed in chapter 6 how I use various characters from TV, movies, and books to help young people understand the concept of personality. I have found that using these common characters is helpful to use with adults due to being recognizable and easy to relate to. I am a firm believer in keeping explanations of personality as simple as possible so that the group members can understand the information and relate it to their lives.

One benefit of working with adults is many have a grasp of personality due to being more cognitively and emotionally mature than adolescents. Adults have more life experience and are usually more self-aware, and I have found many diagnosed with ASD have learned to become keen observers of human behavior. I have found that using TV and movie clips is very useful in demonstrating different personality styles and the way in which those styles either cause conflict with others or create harmony between two people. Individuals diagnosed with ASD are keenly aware of the characters' behaviors in the movie and TV clips, which is encouraging to me and shows that these individuals can learn social behavior and are more observant than people think them to be. The therapist can use personality tests if he or she desires, but I recommend they be quick to administer, simple to take, and easy to understand. I find a simple overview of the four personality types and the various combinations that are usually present in individuals is sufficient so the group members do not become overwhelmed. The goal in learning about personality is to promote a sense of understanding of self and others in order to increase self-confidence and the individual's ability to form relationships with others. Many young adults diagnosed with ASD find themselves entering the workforce for the first time, a potentially confusing and complex social arena. Through being able to understand their own personality as well as identify personality characteristics in another person, some of the confusion can be reduced.

"As Good as It Gets": Personality Types and Social Interactions Galore!

As Good as It Gets (Brooks, 1997), the 1997 film directed by James L. Brooks and starring Jack Nicholson, Helen Hunt, Greg Kinnear, and Cuba Gooding Jr., is a film that contains a great deal of examples of various personality types and a vivid array of social interactions. I have used clips of this film in the past to demonstrate to the group members various personality styles as well as the social interactions that can result from those styles. What I like about this film is that many of the personalities depicted are extreme, such as Marvin played by Jack Nicholson, a somewhat controlling and neurotic individual who is offensive to others. The film contains many characters that can be found in American culture today, such as a single working mother played by Helen Hunt and a gay character named Simon, played by Greg Kinnear, who lives in the same building as Melvin. As the story of the film unfolds, all the characters become intertwined in various ways, and each is thrust into a different role through unfortunate circumstances, creating difficulties for each person involved.

Films such as this are useful not only because of the various personalities and social interactions between people with very different lives, but because it shows how people tend to react when their lives become disrupted. A person can allow disruptions to overwhelm him or her or the person can use the difficult circumstance to grow and change. Adults diagnosed with ASD are often facing huge obstacles in their journey of development and many feel overwhelmed and confused. *As Good as It Gets* (Brooks, 1997) can be inspiring and educational in helping group members realize that while life is full of unexpected challenges, each human being must develop coping skills to get through the difficult times. The film also shows the benefit of humor and how a positive attitude can work wonders in forming relationships and dealing with the uncertainties of everyday life. To effectively use TV and movie clips, a group therapist must know the various challenges group members are experiencing and choose clips that contain the themes with which group members are struggling.

Addressing Problems of Daily Living

I have discussed how adults diagnosed with ASD are often lacking community support and many have only limited, if any, family support. For adults on the autism spectrum who are attempting to navigate a fast-paced world, life can be very overwhelming. The group therapist must be prepared to help adults diagnosed with ASD overcome the challenges of daily living. These challenges may be financial, such as dealing with an unpaid bill or figuring out how to apply for a loan. There may be social challenges, such as dealing with a hostile neighbor or landlord. Challenges may come in the form of logistics such as not knowing how to take the bus or finding transportation to get to a certain location. Other challenges may be getting and preparing food, or needing help with learning basic hygiene, or scheduling appointments with a dentist or doctor. While I do not want to frighten a potential group therapist into thinking he or she is going to have to adopt group members and care for them daily, the therapist should be prepared for some of the above scenarios. There are several ways a therapist can be prepared to assist group members with challenges of daily living.

First, the therapist should be aware of the various support agencies in his or her local community. These agencies, usually connected to a local hospital, church, or government organization, can help an individual with a developmental disability apply for financial assistance, housing, and health care. By having a thorough knowledge of these resources, the therapist can easily direct group members to the various agencies when it is evident that they are in need of services. These agencies usually have information related to transportation, health care, and housing assistance, which is an important resource for those group members who do not have immediate family members who can assist them. The second way a group therapist can prepare to assist group members is by being aware of the various support groups available in the community. Community centers will often provide free classes for learning about free health care, helping with applying for financial assistance, and providing support groups for emotional and mental difficulties, such as dealing with grief or stress. Finally, the group therapist can be of great service to his or her group members by being educated about the various career and employment assistance agencies available in his or her local community. Due to many adults diagnosed with ASD having to enter the workforce in order to live independently, it is important for the therapist to be able to direct group members to agencies that are going to assist them in finding adequate employment. The therapist should be prepared to locate services that not only help with finding employment, but those that assist with career testing and skill development as well. Many adults diagnosed with ASD do not have family members who can help them with finding adequate employment, and the therapist must be able to point group members in the right direction.

The group therapy environment is well suited to provide group members with information that will help when the challenges of daily living arise. The therapist who is prepared to share resources with group members creates a valuable group experience. Through sharing practical knowledge and helping group members find solutions to the challenges of daily living they must face, the therapist also helps to create cohesion amongst group members as well. I find many group members already know the resources available and are more than willing to assist fellow group members with meeting their needs and attaining the appropriate information. Group sessions can be constructed to deal with group members' challenges of daily living and can provide practical help with those challenges. For example, the group therapist may wish to set aside fifteen minutes prior to the session beginning or at the end of the session to discuss various community events or newly discovered resources. Group members should also be given time to share challenges or problems that they are experiencing. This helps not only to develop social skills such as asking for help and communicating about one's needs, but also gives group members the opportunity to help fellow group members, which can foster a sense of empathy and increases perspective-taking.

Epilogue

Writing for me is always a remarkable experience, and working on this book has been an extraordinary one. Putting this book together has again reminded me of what an honor it is to work with children, adolescents, and adults diagnosed with ASD. I feel a great sense of gratitude to be part of a profession that seeks to help these individuals better understand themselves and empower them to reach their full potential. Group therapy with individuals diagnosed with ASD is a rich experience, and I hope it is evident the effectiveness of this approach extends far beyond behavior modification or teaching social skills. As the numbers of those diagnosed with ASD continues to grow, group therapy will continue to be an important part of the treatment landscape. Skilled therapists will be in demand to lead these groups and create an atmosphere of warmth, acceptance, respect, and safety, so individuals diagnosed with ASD can heal, learn, and grow. Will the journey be easy? No, nothing worthwhile ever is. Is the developmental journey of these remarkable individuals easy? No, but those of us who work with them can help pull them up the developmental ladder by bringing hope and light through the unique experience group therapy provides. I invite you to be a part of this distinct and effective form of therapy and hope you are as inspired as I am as we look towards a bright and exciting future of learning and helping those on the autism spectrum.

Dr. Kevin B. Hull
July 27, 2013
Lakeland, Florida

Appendix

Quick Reference Guide

CHAPTER TWO: ADDITIONAL CHARACTERISTICS OF ASD

Specified Interests

Intense preoccupation with interests that are unique to the individual. The interest can at times cause problems in relationships due to the intensity and tendency of the individual to have difficulty directing his or her attention to anything other than the specified interest. Specified interests can be used in the therapy process as a way to build rapport with the group member in addition to increasing social interactions and building up a sense of value and self-worth.

Odd Conversation Style

A stiff, plodding, one-sided conversation style which may make the individual appear as though he or she is selfish or rude. The individual may not know how to respond to questions or compliments and may not respond at all. This style of conversation often stems from the individual's difficulty to sense how he or she sounds and appears to others. (See Mindblindness).

Empathy Restriction

An appearance of a lack of empathy. Those diagnosed with ASD may be perceived as "mechanical" or "robot-like." While the individual may appear this way, it is important to note that this does not mean those diagnosed with ASD do not possess empathy or are uncaring. It is simply a matter of them not knowing how to show it.

Pessimistic World View

A seemingly negative, pessimistic view of the world around them. Due to seeing the world as "black and white" individuals often come across as negative, but in reality most are simply realists and do not waste energy on the "fluff" that society teaches and neurotypical individuals tend to naturally adopt.

Mindblindness

A lack of an ability to see a situation from a different perspective, also known as Theory of Mind (ToM). Deficiencies in perspective-taking or ToM make it hard for the individuals to form close, personal relationships and can make them appear to have a lack of empathy. A lack of perspective-taking makes it hard for the individual diagnosed with ASD to predict the intentions or motives of others, resulting in social and relational problems.

Alexithymia

An inability to recognize and give meaning to emotions in oneself and others. The inability to understand emotions or put them into words can make the individual appear cold or uncaring. Alexithymia creates difficulty in forming relationships due to the difficulty the individual has in understanding the emotional reactions of others. The individual diagnosed with ASD tends to be confused by emotions and can have extreme difficulty putting feelings into words.

CHAPTER THREE: YALOM'S (2005) THERAPEUTIC FACTORS THAT MAKE GROUP THERAPY EFFECTIVE

- Instillation of Hope
- Universality
- Imparting Information
- Altruism
- The Corrective Recapitalization of the Primary Family Group
- Development of Socializing Techniques
- Imitative Behavior
- Interpersonal Learning
- Group Cohesiveness
- Catharsis
- Existential Factors

Group Therapy's Effectiveness with Those on the Autism Spectrum

- Teaching Social Skills
- Overcoming Alexithymia
- Increasing Perspective-Taking
- Increasing Self-Worth and Self-Confidence
- Establishing a Sense of Identity

CHAPTER FOUR: GROUP THERAPY TECHNIQUES WITH YOUNG CHILDREN

Emotions: Identification and Understanding

The Colors of Emotions—What are Emotions?

Assigning different colors to represent the various emotions children can form a mental picture of an emotion which will lead to learning how to effectively express and deal with the emotion. For example, the color "red" is used as a representation of anger, which gives the child a way to tell a parent or caregiver about how he is feeling, and leads the parent to help the child verbalize the feeling. (Child: "I'm feeling really "red" right now, mom." Mom: "That means you are really angry; tell me what you're angry about.")

From Colors to Coping

Once emotions are represented by the various colors, coping tools are given to help group members learn to deal with the negative emotions. Group members are prompted to discuss instances where they felt out of control but did not react negatively or violently.

Emotional Coping Skills—A Balloon Game to Teach Breathing Techniques

Balloons are used to give group members the sensation of slow, full, methodical breathing. After two or three rounds of blowing up the balloon, it is then released as a picture of getting rid of negative emotion due to staying calm through good breathing.

Board Games to Help Learn to Deal with Frustration

A variety of board games can be used to help young children diagnosed with ASD learn to deal with frustration that often leads to impulse control problems. Operation, Trouble, Hungry Hippos, and Candy Land are just a few that are useful. When a group member begins to get upset, the therapist can prompt him or her to use a coping tool to self-soothe. Board games provide group members with real-world situations in which they can practice techniques that will generalize to the child's life outside of the group.

Group Sand Play

Sand play is useful to help build cohesion in the group. Members gain a sense of togetherness when working towards a unified goal. The therapist may assign group members to work on a specific task, such as building a structure. A "foreman" is assigned and gives orders to the other group members who serve at various building stations. Each member rotates through the various stations and takes a turn at being "in charge." Group members may also play out certain scenarios, such as overcoming bullying or creating a landscape that represents a certain place. Free play can also be used in which the group members are introduced to the sand tray and allowed to freely experiment with the medium.

Group LEGO® Play

Similar to group sand play, LEGO® play can be used in a structured organized manner in which group members take on various roles (i.e. foreman, builder, supplier, etc.) or a free play format that is unstructured. This technique is useful to build stronger social connections between group members and is helpful in building a sense of self-worth and self-confidence.

LEGO® Mini-Figures

LEGO® mini-figures are useful in helping to teach social skills, model appropriate behavior, explain personality, as well as providing a child with a way to represent him or herself. Mini-figures allow children to play out scenarios that may be stressful for them, such as dealing with a bullying situation or a problem at home. Mini-figure play can also help increase a sense of self-worth and self-confidence through playing out scenarios in which the child must take a risk and overcome the feeling of fear.

Increasing Perspective-Taking in Younger Children

Follow the Leader

The classic game creates a scenario in which another person's behavior and mannerisms must be copied by group members. This technique is helpful in increasing joint attention, which is a common deficit in those diagnosed with ASD. The "leader" also must assume a leadership role which can help increase his or her sense of self-worth.

The PEZ Game

Similar to the technique that involves using LEGO® mini-figures, the PEZ game teaches perspective-taking through a child playing out the role of a character and forces the child to see a situation from a different perspective. The game is also useful in explaining personality and allows group members to practice interacting with each other through a fun and playful manner.

Video/Computer Games

Video/Computer games can be used to increase perspective-taking through watching a peer play (through practicing joint attention) as well as through playing as a certain character, like Spiderman or Harry Potter. This technique also teaches a variety of social skills, such as waiting in line for one's turn, or congratulating another player when he or she does well. Conversely, the technique also helps members learn to not taunt or jeer when someone fails, as this is hurtful and not socially appropriate. For younger children, Super Mario Bros. and the LEGO® series of games are useful to use in a group format, as well as the Wii and XBOX 360 Kinect.

Story-Telling and Role-Play

Story-telling and role-play allows group members to practice taking on a different role as well as putting thoughts and feelings into words. Each story-teller also practices getting up in front of a group which is frightening for many individuals, both neurotypical and those on the autism spectrum.

Thought-Bubble Training

Thought-Bubble Training is useful to help young children begin practicing imagining what other people might be thinking. This training helps increase a child's perspective-taking ability and also lays the ground work to pull the child up the developmental ladder as the child matures mentally and emotionally.

Increasing Self-Worth and Self-Awareness in Younger Children

Show and Tell

This classic age-old technique is useful in promoting a sense of self-worth through the child being able to show and talk about something that is dear to her. The other group members also get to work on skills of listening and joint attention while the "expert" is telling and showing.

I am Unique

This technique involves the therapist drawing a figure to represent the child, complete with the various personality characteristics, specified interests, and mannerisms that make the child truly unique. Once these are written down, the child can talk about himself and share the various characteristics with the group. The goal is that the child gains self-awareness and the child's sense of self-worth is increased.

Be the Teacher!

Similar to "Show and Tell," this technique allows the child to teach fellow group members about her specified interest. The teaching may be simply sharing facts, or it may be showing fellow group members how to make something. Through this technique, the child experiences an increased sense of self-worth and also gets to practice being in a leadership role; group members are able to practice social skills and joint attention.

Pass the Ball!

This technique is a good way to start group therapy sessions to get children acclimated to the process of listening while another person is talking and waiting for their turn. The child who is sharing about himself also experiences an increased sense of self-worth and learns to listen to others in a group setting.

Group Sand/LEGO® Play

Group sand and LEGO® play are useful to help raise a child's sense of self-worth and self-awareness through giving the child the opportunity to take on a different role and play out scenarios that are problematic. For example, group members may play out a bullying scenario with LEGO® mini-figures and gain a sense of self-awareness through interacting with other group members who are experiencing the same situation.

Bullying Prevention and Younger Children: Physical Tools

Getting to Safety!

This technique teaches group members to use physical force when in a situation where they are physically threatened. Many children who are bullied get cornered in bathrooms or hallways in which teachers are not present, and many children on the autism spectrum do not realize the amount of force they she can generate to push past the bully and get to safety.

Tell an Adult!

While it seems obvious, many children diagnosed with ASD tend to internalize their terror and anger when bullied instead of telling their parents or a teacher. Reminding them of the need to tell an adult helps reinforce to young children how important it is to let adults know when they are being bullied.

Bullying and Younger Children: Mental Tools

Think Powerful! I Don't Have to Let Someone Hurt Me!

This cognitive tool challenges younger children to change their thinking from a victim-like and powerless stance to a strength-based and intentional mindset. Based on the idea that one's thinking influences one's feelings and behavior, this technique lays groundwork for future cognitive work as the child experiences mental and emotional growth.

Think Smart! "I Can Get Help—I'm Not Alone!"

Another cognitive-based tool, this technique works to instill a pattern of positive, truth-based thoughts that lead to positive, intentional behavior. The technique also reinforces the fact that the child is not alone in her struggle and that she can get help from peers and teachers alike.

Bullying and Younger Children: Emotional Tools

Overcoming Fear!

Helping group members overcome fear that results from bullying is an important part of teaching children diagnosed with ASD to be emotionally strong. Learning to self-soothe and having an "Escape Plan" are parts of teaching group members to overcome paralyzing fear.

Using Anger as Positive Energy!

This technique teaches younger children to learn to use anger as a positive motivating force to make choices that are positive and intentional. Children can learn to use anger to overcome fear or do something that they love instead of turning the anger inward which results in self-loathing and possibly self-harm. Bubble-breathing and role-play can be helpful in teaching this valuable technique.

CHAPTER FOUR: GROUP THERAPY TECHNIQUES WITH OLDER CHILDREN

Emotional Tools

The Use of UNO to Understand Emotions

This technique uses the different colors of the card game UNO to help group members understand the various emotions and lays a foundation for future learning about coping with negative emotions. This technique is also valuable in getting young people diagnosed with ASD to understand sadness and be able to talk about it.

The Worry Can

The "Worry Can" is a useful technique that offers group members a visual representation of overcoming worries and fear. This technique also teaches the group members the important process of expressing a fear both verbally and in writing and provides a visual representation of throwing the fear away. This helps to provide a sense of empowerment and provides a pathway of seeing a negative emotion from a different point of view.

Balloon Breathing, Nice and Slow!

A great technique to teach young people how deep breathing is the first step in becoming physically and emotionally grounded and reducing the effects of "fight-or-flight."

Games to Help Deal with Frustration

"Bop-It! Smash!" (Special Edition) is a valuable game that helps older children learn to be non-reactive when feeling frustration. This game is a fun and innovative way to learn to overcome frustration through concentration and ignoring negative comments of others.

Video/Computer Games

Video/Computer games provide valuable tools in teaching older children to overcome negative emotions such as anger, frustration, and fear. Through game play, group members can feel negative emotions and use the tools provided by the group therapist to learn to be non-reactive and self-soothe. Games such as MineCraft, and skill games such as those on the XBOX 360 Kinect or Wii Sports, put group members in real-time situations that force them to deal with the frustration and anger that comes from failure and losing.

Older Children and Perspective-Taking

Thought-Bubble Training

Similar to the technique that was discussed with younger children, Thought-Bubble Training is useful to get older children diagnosed with ASD to imagine what another person may be thinking.

Shoe-Switch Game

This technique uses a visual representation of actually stepping into another's shoes. The therapist can also draw an outline of each group member's shoes and have the members imagine being "in another's shoes." The point of this technique is to get group members to think about seeing a situation from another person's shoes and imagine what another person might be thinking.

Computer/Video Game Play

Video/Computer games are useful in helping older children improve their perspective-taking ability. Through watching how other children play, which helps with practicing joint attention, group members can imagine how another person thinks. The therapist has the ability to stop the action at any time and can point out the differences in group members' play, and also explain how each person thinks and feels differently.

Increasing Self-Worth and Self-Awareness in Older Children

Show and Tell

Similar to the technique with younger children, "Show and Tell" for older children contains valuable social skill teaching such as speaking firmly and plainly, making eye contact with one's audience and answering questions from audience members. This is a good technique for those diagnosed with ASD who have an extreme aversion to talking in front of a group.

Pass the Ball

A good ice-breaker, this technique also helps with grounding group members physically, mentally, and emotionally after a long school day and transitioning between school or home and the group therapy setting.

The Slow Motion Game

The "Slow Motion Game" presents a variety of physical activities that are done in "slow motion" in order to help older children who struggle with impulsivity gain better self-control. This technique also helps young people on the autism spectrum become more aware of their bodies and the motion that is generated by their body. A CBT component can be added by "freezing" the action and asking group members what they are thinking in the middle of the behavior.

Bullying Prevention for Older Children: Physical Tools

Getting to Safety! Red Light, Green Light

A simple game that helps young people learn to use their senses and control impulsivity, this technique seeks to help young people on the autism spectrum become more aware of their bodies and the energy that body movement generates. This also directs group members to direct their gaze to the eyes of the "leader." This game also helps group members learn to make quick and decisive body movements, which is helpful since many young people on the autism spectrum become "frozen" when bullied.

Give Your Therapist a Good Shove!

Similar to the technique that was used with younger children, this technique helps young people diagnosed with ASD become familiar with their bodily force and teaches them to direct that energy to a positive action when cornered by a bully.

Sword Fights: Be Bold and Ready for Action!

Foam swords are used to build self-confidence and body awareness. Rules are set to ensure safety. This technique also helps young people develop impulse control, body awareness, and a sense of bodily force.

Bullying Prevention for Older Children: Mental Tools

Devise a Safety Plan!

This technique forces young people to mentally picture a bullying scenario and then create a plan to get away from the situation and move towards safety. Group members are asked to walk through the steps from beginning to end and memorize their "Safety Plan" in order to put it into action.

Think Powerful! Think Smart!

Based on the CBT approach that thoughts dictate one's emotions and behaviors, this technique introduces group members to the power of positive, truth-based thinking that leads to intentional and strong behavior.

Bullying Prevention in Older Children: Emotional Tools

Comic Book Stories: "With Great Power There Must Also Come Great Responsibility"

This technique uses the medium of comic books and Manga to help group members familiarize themselves with emotions and then drawing out or writing scenarios in which the young person overcomes the negative emotion and uses it as positive energy.

Getting Rid of Shame Game

Based on CBT, this technique introduces group members to identifying underlying thoughts that are causing feelings of shame that arise after a bullying incident. Through the use of a white board and erasers, group members practice using truth-based thinking in order to "wipe away" feelings of shame. This technique can also create discussion of group members' bullying experiences and coming up with solutions for those who are experiencing ongoing bullying.

CHAPTER SIX: GROUP THERAPY TECHNIQUES WITH ADOLESCENTS

Emotions: Identification and Understanding

Recognizing Emotions in Others: Using Media

The use of TV or movie clips helps group members learn to identify various emotions in other people. The goal is that the knowledge gained from watching examples in TV and movie clips will generalize to group members being able to learn to identify emotions in those around them.

Putting Feelings into Words

A technique that focuses on helping young people articulate what they are feeling, "Putting Feelings into Words" is a valuable teaching tool as it walks group members through the process of creating explanations for the feelings that they are experiencing. This technique is helpful as it provides a valuable alternative, for those on the autism spectrum impulsively react or shut down and have difficulty with articulation of emotions.

Increasing Perspective-Taking

Video/Computer Games

The games are used to help group members imagine what another is thinking while watching peers play a game, which also helps increase joint attention. Games such as the Sims or MineCraft are useful to help increase perspective-taking in adolescents diagnosed with ASD.

TV and Movie Clips

TV and films are representations of real-life scenarios and are useful to help group members practice interpreting another's thoughts and behaviors. Clips are chosen that contain themes that are similar to the situations that group members can relate to, such as home/family or the school environment.

Thought-Bubble Training

A useful way to help group members imagine what another person is thinking, Thought-Bubble Training can be fun and informative in teaching individuals diagnosed with ASD a valuable skill.

Increasing Self-Worth and Self-Awareness

Self-Worth Exercises

Designed to increase group members' sense of self-worth and self-awareness, this technique helps individuals examine gifts, talents, and personal attributes that make them unique and special. This technique can also include a perspective-taking and empathy component in which group members share thoughts about each other's gifts and talents.

Personality: A Pathway to Self-Awareness and Awareness of Others

This technique helps teach group members the basic four personality types in order to better understand themselves and to learn to understand others. Through the use of recognizable characters from cartoons and comics, group members learn how personality influences relationships. A valuable addition to this technique is teaching group members to work through conflicts.

Bullying Prevention Techniques for Adolescents

A Narrative Approach

Narrative therapy is a powerful approach to help individuals see a problem from a different vantage point, which helps to increase coping skills and strengthens resolve towards overcoming the problem. This process involves information gathering, journaling, and writing a story in which the problem is resolved and the challenges overcome by the individual. The story can be told through writing, drawing, or acting out the solutions to the problem. Narrative approaches are useful with individuals diagnosed with ASD to help with putting feelings into words and learning coping skills to deal with stress and challenges of daily living, such as dealing with bullying behavior.

Getting Dramatic: The Power of Acting Out Traumatic Events

Drama therapy is a powerful way to help adolescents overcome the emotional and mental effects of bullying. Group members learn coping skills through role-play and through observing the positive coping skills of others. Drama therapy helps young people put thoughts and feelings into words and develop behaviors that are positive and intentional. The drama therapy process involves "brainstorming," story development, acting, and debriefing/de-roling. Drama therapy is especially helpful in helping individuals diagnosed with ASD work through negative emotions that arise from bullying situations.

CHAPTER SEVEN: GROUP THERAPY TECHNIQUES WITH ADULTS

Clinical Considerations

Addressing Varying Developmental Levels

The group therapist must be aware of the developmental differences of group members and tailor the goals and focus of the group with these differences in mind.

Setting Flexible Group Goals

Goal setting is an important part of structuring a group with individual adults diagnosed with ASD; however, due to the characteristics of ASD the group therapist will need to create goals that are flexible as the needs and challenges of group members become apparent.

Safety

The group therapist must work hard to create an environment of safety in the group therapy environment. Due to the diverse needs and unique characteristics of group members, the individual's sense of safety will vary from member to member. The group therapist must be aware of each group member's needs and emotional makeup in order to ensure he or she is doing everything possible to create a warm, accepting, and safe environment for group members.

Concurrent Group and Individual Therapy

Group therapy members may also be attending individual sessions concurrently. It is important that the group therapist maintain communication with the individual therapist so that group and individual goals align. For the therapist seeing a client in group and individual therapy concurrently, he or she must work hard to safeguard confidentiality and not betray the client's sense of safety and freedom as a result of the therapist having access to a great deal of information about the client.

Emotions: Identification and Understanding

Teaching Group Members to Self-Soothe

Helping group members learn to self-soothe and shift from sympathetic to parasympathetic functioning increases coping skills through the individual being able to access logical and rational thinking processes. This practical and simple exercise is a wonderful tool to give individuals diagnosed with ASD in order to overcome stress and negative emotions.

Relaxation Techniques

Deep breathing, journaling, positive imagery, yoga, and exercise are all techniques that group members can learn to combat the effects of negative emotions that come from stress.

Recognizing and Identifying Emotions in Others

Thought-Bubble Training and using TV and movie clips are useful ways to help group members increase their ability to identify and interpret the emotions and thoughts of others. Through the use of these techniques, group members can improve their sense of self-confidence and relationship-building skills.

Relationship-Building Skills

Conversation: It's Sort of like Ping-Pong

Using the visual representation of a game of Ping-Pong or tennis helps group members visualize the back-and-forth elements of conversations. This mental picture can help them when feeling "stuck" in attempting to converse with others, and reminds them to allow others to respond to questions so that the individual diagnosed with ASD is not dominating the conversation.

Specified Interests as Relationship Builders

This technique emphasizes a group member's specified interest as a way for him or her to meet new people and social groups.

Role-Play: Practicing the Art of Forming Relationships

Through role-play, group members learn to make conversation, practice giving socially appropriate responses, and learn how to share thoughts and feelings in real-world scenarios. This technique is based on the idea that all humans must practice socializing behavior before becoming adept in navigating social landscapes. Group members are provided with a fun and non-stressful approach to learn valuable skills.

Field Trips

Field trips place group members in real-world scenarios and encourage them to use the skills gained in the group therapy environment to interact and navigate various social landscapes. An excellent technique for those group members who are agoraphobic and insecure, the peer group can provide a sense of safety and encouragement to help the person face their fears.

Personality and Adults Diagnosed with ASD

Who Am I and Who Are You?

Based on the techniques explained in chapter 6, this technique helps group members understand the basics of personality and use that knowledge to build stronger relationships and learn how to work through conflict with others.

"As Good as It Gets" Personality Types and Social Interactions Galore!

As Good as It Gets is an example of a film that is useful in helping group members learn about personalities and observe a variety of social interactions.

Addressing Problems of Daily Living

The therapist should be aware of various community resources that can help individuals diagnosed with ASD meet and overcome the challenges of daily living. Many adults diagnosed with ASD struggle in the areas of finance, health care, and transportation. A skilled group therapist seeks out resources to help in these areas and shares this information with his or her group members in order to aid them in adapting to adult life as an individual on the autism spectrum.

References

American Psychiatric Association: *Diagnostic and Statistical Manual of Mental Disorders, Fifth Edition*. Washington, DC, American Psychiatric Association, 2013.

Attwood, T. (1998). *Asperger's syndrome: A guide for parents and professionals*. London: Jessica Kingsley

Attwood , T. (2004). Cognitive behaviour therapy for children and adults with Asperger's syndrome. *Behaviour Change, 21,* 147–181. doi: 10.1375/bech.21.3.147.55995

Attwood, T. (2007). *The complete guide to Asperger's syndrome*. London England: Jessica Kingsley Publishers.

Badenoch, B. & Bogdan, N. (2012). Safety and connection: The neurobiology of play. In L. Gallo-Lopez and L. C. Rubin (Eds.), *Play-based interventions for children and adolescents with autism apectrum disorders* (pp. 3–18). New York: Routledge/Taylor & Francis Group.

Baron-Cohen, S. (2000). Is Asperger syndrome/high functioning autism necessarily a disability? *Development and Psychopathology, 12,* 489–500.

Bell, L. G., & Bell, D. C. (2005). Family dynamics in adolescence affect midlife well-being. *Journal of Family Psychology, 19*(2), 198-207. doi:10.1037/0893-3200.19.2.198

Bromfield, R. (2010). *Doing therapy with children and adolescents with Asperger syndrome*. Hoboken, NJ US: John Wiley & Sons Inc.

Brooks, J. (Director). (1997). *As good as it gets*. (Motion picture). United States: TriStar Pictures/Gracie Films.

Bundy-Myrow, S. (2012). Family theraplay: Connecting with children on the autism spectrum. In L. Gallo-Lopez & L. Rubin (Eds.), *Play-based interventions for children and adolescents with autism spectrum disorders* (pp. 137–157). New York: Routledge/Taylor & Francis Group.

Cabe, N. (2001). Relaxation training: Bubble breaths. In H. Kaduson and C. Schaefer (Eds.), *101 More favorite play therapy techniques* (p. 346–349). Lanham, MD: Jason Aronson.

Carter, S. (2009). Bullying of students with Asperger syndrome. *Issues In Comprehensive Pediatric Nursing, 32*(3), 145–154. doi:10.1080/01460860903062782

Cashin, A. (2008). Narrative therapy: A psychotherapeutic approach in the treatment of adolescents with Asperger's disorder. *Journal of Child and Adolescent Psychiatric Nursing, 21,* 48-56. doi: 10.1111/j.1744-6171.2008.00128.x

Cashin, A., Browne, G., Bradbury, J. & Mulder, A. (2013). The effectiveness of narrative therapy with young people with autism. *Journal of Child and Adolescent Psychiatric Nursing, 26:* 32–41. doi: 10.1111/jcap.12020

Charman, T., Swettenham, J., Baron-Cohen, S., Cox, A., Baird, G., & Drew, A. (1997). Infants with autism: An investigation of empathy, pretend play, joint attention, and imitation. *Developmental Psychology, 33*(5), 781–789. doi:10.1037/0012-1649.33.5.781

Courtney, J. A. (2012). Touching autism through developmental play therapy. In L. Gallo-Lopez & L. Rubin (Eds.), *Play-based interventions for children and adolescents with autism spectrum disorders* (pp. 137–157). New York: Routledge/Taylor & Francis Group.

Erikson, E. H. (1963). *Childhood and society.* New York: Norton.

Fanning, E., Brighton, C. (2007). The Sims in therapy: An examination of feasibility and potential of the use of game-based learning in clinical practice. In B. K. Weiderhold, G. Riva, S. Bouchard (Eds.), *Annual Review of Cybertherapy and Telemedicine: Advanced Technologies in the Behavioral, Social, and Neurosciences,* 5, 1–11. ISSN: 1554-8716.

Frith, U. (1991). *Autism and Asperger syndrome*. Cambridge: Cambridge University Press.

Ghaziuddin, M., Ghaziuddin, N., & Greden, J. (2002). Depression in persons with autism: Implications for research and clinical care. *Journal of Autism and Developmental Disorders*, 32(4), 299–306. doi:10.1023/A:1016330802348

Gillberg, C. (1991) Clinical and neurobiological aspects of Asperger's syndrome in six families studied. In *Autism and Asperger's syndrome* (ed. U. Frith), pp. 122–146. Cambridge: Cambridge University Press.

Hall, T. M., Kaduson, H., and Schaefer, C. E. (2002). "Fifteen effective play therapy techniques." *Professional Psychology: Research and Practice,* 33(6), 515–22. doi:10.1037/0735–7028.33.6.515.

Hess, E. (2012). DIR floortime: A developmental/relational play therapy approach for treating children impacted by autism. In L. Gallo-Lopez & L. Rubin (Eds.), *Play-based interventions for children and adolescents with autism spectrum disorders* (pp. 137–157). New York: Routledge/Taylor & Francis Group.

Hoberman, H. M., Lewinsohn, P. M., & Tilson, M. (1988). Group treatment of depression: Individual predictors of outcome. *Journal of Consulation of Clinical Psychology*, 56, 393–398.

Hull, K. (2009). Computer/video games as a play therapy tool in reducing emotional disturbances in children. *Dissertation Abstracts International,* 70.

Hull, K. (2011). *Play therapy and Asperger's syndrome: Helping children and adolescents grow, connect, and heal through the art of play.* Lanham, MD: Jason Aronson.

Irving, L. M., Snyder, C. R., Cheavens, J., Gravel, L. Hanke, J., Hilberg, P., & Nelson, N. (2004). The relationship between hope and outcomes at the pre-treatment, beginning, and later phases of psychotherapy. *Journal of Psychotherapy Integration*, 14, 419–443.

Josselyn, I.M. The ego in adolescence. *American Journal of Orthopsychiatry*, 24: 223–227,1954.

Klin , A. Volkmar , F.R. (1995). Asperger's syndrome guidelines for assessment and diagnosis. Yale child study center, New Haven, Connecticut: Learning Disabilities Association of America.

LeGoff, D. B. (2004). Use of LEGO®© as a therapeutic medium for improving social competence. *Journal of Autism and Developmental Disorders*, 34(5), 557–571. doi:10.1007/s10803-004-2550-0

McGuire, A. E., & Michalko, R. (2011). Minds between us: Autism, mindblindness and the uncertainty of communication. *Educational Philosophy & Theory*, *43*(2), 162–177. doi:10.1111/j.1469-5812.2009.00537.x

Munro, J. (2010). An integrated model of psychotherapy for teens and adults with Asperger syndrome. *Journal of Systemic Therapies*, 29(3), 82-96. doi:10.1521/jsyt.2010.29.3.82

Owens, G. Granader, Y. Humphrey, A. Baron-Cohen, S. (2008). LEGO® ® therapy and the social use of language program: An evaluation of two social skills interventions for children with high-functioning autism and Asperger's syndrome. *Journal of Autism and Developmental Disorders* 38: 1944-57. doi: 10.1007/s10803-008-0590-6

Paynter, J., Peterson, C. C. (2013). Further evidence of benefits of thought-bubble training for theory of mind development in children with autism spectrum disorders. *Research in Autism Spectrum Disorders, 7(2): 344–348.*

Rao, P. A., Beidel, D. C., & Murray, M. J. (2008). Social skills interventions for children with Asperger's syndrome or high-functioning autism: A review and recommendations. *Journal Of Autism And Developmental Disorders*, *38*(2), 353-361. doi:10.1007/s10803-007-0402-4

Ray, D. C., Sullivan, J. M., and Carlson, S. E. (2012). Relational intervention: Child-centered play therapy with children on the autism spectrum. In L. Gallo-Lopez & L. Rubin (Eds.), *Play-based interventions for children and adolescents with autism spectrum disorders* (pp. 19–35). New York: Routledge/Taylor & Francis Group.

Richardson, J. F. (2012). The world of the sand tray and the child on the autism spectrum. In L. Gallo-Lopez & L. Rubin (Eds.), *Play-based interventions for children and adolescents with autism spectrum disorders* (pp. 137–157). New York: Routledge/Taylor & Francis Group.

Robison, J. E. (2007). *Look me in the eye: My life with Asperger's.* New York: Three Rivers Press.

Rubin, L. C. (2012). Playing on the autism spectrum. In L. Gallo-Lopez & L. Rubin (Eds.), *Play-based interventions for children and adolescents with autism spectrum disorders* (pp. 19–35). New York: Routledge/Taylor & Francis Group.

Samson , A. C. Huber , O. Gross , J. J. (2012). Emotion regulation in Asperger's syndrome and high-functioning autism. *Emotion, 12*, 659–665. doi: 10.1037/a0027975

Sayers, J. M. (2007). The Incredible Hulk and emotional literacy. In L. C. Rubin (Ed.), *Using superheroes in counseling and play therapy* (pp. 89–101). New York: Springer Publishing Company, LLC.

Schmidt, C., Heybyrne, B. (2004). *Autism in the school aged child: Expanding behavioral strategies and promoting success.* Denver, CO: Autism Family Press.

Schultz, D. F. (2005). *A language of the heart: Therapy stories that heal.* Florida: Rainbow Books.

Skigen, D. (2008). Taking the sand tray high tech: Using the Sims as a therapeutic tool in the treatment of adolescents. In L. C. Rubin, L. C. Rubin (Eds.), *Popular culture in counseling, psychotherapy, and play-based interventions* (pp. 165–179). New York: Springer Publishing Co.

Snyder, C. R., Parenteau, S. C., Shorey, H. S., Kahle, K. E., Berg, C. (2002). Hope as the underlying process in the psychotherapeutic change process. *International Gestalt Journal, 25*, 11–29.

Sword (Foam) http://www.wikihow.com/Make-a-Boffer-(Foam-Sword)

Taylor, G. J., Bagby, R., & Parker, J. (1997). *Disorders of affect regulation: Alexithymia in medical and psychiatric illness.* New York: Cambridge University Press. doi:10.1017/CBO9780511526831

Tricomi, L. P., & Gallo-Lopez, L. (2012). The ACT project: Enhancing social competence through drama therapy and performance. In L. Gallo-Lopez and L. C. Rubin (Eds.), *Play-based interventions for children and adolescents with autism spectrum disorders* (pp. 271–291). New York: Routledge/Taylor & Francis Group.

Tuason, M. T., & Friedlander, M. L. (2000). Do parents' differentiation levels predict those of their adult children? and other tests of Bowen theory in a Philippine sample. *Journal of Counseling Psychology, 47*(1), 27–35. doi:10.1037/0022-0167.47.1.27

Volkmar, F. R., Klin, A., Siegel, B., & Szatmari, P. (1994). Field trial for autistic disorder in DSM-IV. *The American Journal of Psychiatry, 151*(9), 1361–1367.

Weber, K. (2008). Asperger's syndrome: From hiding to thriving. *Nurse Practitioner*: July 2008 33(7), 14-21. doi: 10.1097/01.NPR.0000325974.78130.72

Wellman , H. M. Baron-Cohen , S. Caswell , R. Gomez , J. C. Swettenham , J. Toye , E., Lagattuta , K. (2002). Thought-bubbles help children with autism acquire an alternative to a theory of mind. *Autism*, 6, 343–363.

Wellman, H. M., & Peterson, C. C. (2013). Deafness, thought bubbles, and theory-of-mind development. *Developmental Psychology. Advance online publication.* doi:10.1037/a0032419.

Wing, L. (1981). Asperger's syndrome: A clinical account. *Psychological Medicine: A Journal of Research in Psychiatry and the Allied Sciences,* 11(1), 15–129.

Yalom, I. D., & Leszez, M. (2005). *The theory and practice of group psychotherapy (5th ed.).* New York: Basic Books.

Index

About the Author

Kevin B. Hull, PhD, LMHC, owns a private counseling practice in Lakeland, Florida, where he has practiced for the past thirteen years. He conducts individual and group therapy with children, adolescents, and adults on the autism spectrum. Prior to working in private practice, he worked in numerous community mental health settings in central Florida. He has taught at the graduate level for ten years and currently is a professor for Liberty University Online Masters of Counseling program.

www.ingramcontent.com/pod-product-compliance
Ingram Content Group UK Ltd.
Pitfield, Milton Keynes, MK11 3LW, UK
UKHW012041150926
475560UK00001B/132